CHICAGO

CHICAGO

With the *Chicago Tribune* Articles
That Inspired It
by Maurine Watkins

Edited and with an
Introduction by
Thomas H. Pauly

SOUTHERN ILLINOIS UNIVERSITY PRESS
Carbondale and Edwardsville

The publisher gratefully acknowledges the cooperation
of the DePaul University Libraries in providing the
text of *Chicago* that was used for the present edition.

Library of Congress Cataloging-in-Publication Data

Watkins, Maurine.
Chicago : with the Chicago tribune articles that inspired it / by
Maurine Watkins ; edited and with an introduction by Thomas H. Pauly.
p.   cm.
Reprint of the play Chicago, originally published in 1927, with the
author's newspaper articles of the criminal trials that inspired it.

1. City and town life—Illinois—Chicago—Drama. 2. Criminals—
Illinois—Chicago—Drama. I. Pauly, Thomas H. II. Title.
PS3545.A828C5 1997
812'.52—dc21   97-10047
ISBN 0-8093-2129-7 (pbk. : alk. paper)   CIP

CONTENTS

INTRODUCTION

Chicago premiered in New York City on December 30, 1926. The reviews were favorable and the comedy enjoyed a prosperous run of 172 performances, which was followed by a successful tour of several other big cities and a well-received movie version.[1] Its thirty-year-old author, Maurine Watkins, emerged as the show's star and was much photographed and profiled.[2] This young woman, who had come from the heartland Midwest and had honed her skills in George Pierce Baker's playwriting class at the newly founded Yale School of Drama, was the toast of New York for her rollicking indictment of Chicago, New York City's commercial and cultural rival. However, her blaze of glory proved only a flash. After several assignments for New York newspapers and a disappointing reception of her next play, Watkins went to work in Hollywood but had little success. Sometime around 1940, she rejoined her parents in Florida, there faded into obscurity, and died in 1969.[3]

Though never forgotten, her comedy has not fared much better. Published only once in 1927 when Alfred Knopf thought it important enough to have it launch "The Theatre of Today— a library of plays significant in the development of modern drama,"[4] *Chicago* has never been republished and has now been out of print for almost seventy years. In 1942, Warner Brothers made a second movie of the play, retitling it *Roxie Hart* and starring Ginger Rogers. This represented an attempt to capitalize on the success of *His Girl Friday* (1940), a remake of *Front Page* (1928), with Rosalind Russell cast in the lead role of Hildy Johnson. Though *Roxie Hart* kept *Chicago* alive, it reinforced the long-standing assumption that *Front Page* was a superior creation and obscured the fact that *Chicago* was the original and *Front Page* the variation.

During the 1950s and 1960s, several Broadway producers became interested in converting *Chicago* into a musical. However, their plans foundered upon Watkins's reluctance to sell the necessary rights. Only after her death in 1969 when her estate finally released the rights were Bob Fosse and Gwen Verdon able to team up with Fred Ebb and John Kraft and proceed with their musical version that reached Broadway in 1975, almost twenty years after its original conception.[5] Though upstaged by the opening of *Chorus Line* the same season, it overcame mixed reviews and enjoyed a successful run. Consequently, both the *Chicago* that occasionally plays at regional theaters and the recent Broadway hit involve the Fosse musical.

That Maurine Watkins and her comedy should be so forgotten today is almost amazing in view of all the attention recently lavished on the trials of Amy Fisher, the Menendez brothers, and O. J. Simpson. Watkins's play offers a bracing reminder that lurid crimes were as aggressively commercialized seventy years ago as they are today. As we grow uneasily aware of the hyperbole and hypocrisy in our media's exploitation of yet another trial, *Chicago* demonstrates that similar conditions have existed for most of the twentieth century. Even better, Watkins's comedy ridicules these conditions and exposes folly far more effectively than the standard complaints about our media-crazed society. Her comic depiction of a woman groping toward liberation and the future foregrounds pressures women still face, but it is downright uncanny in its anticipation of today's news-as-entertainment culture.

The play's brief opening scene presents the audience with the hard truth of the outraged Roxie angrily shooting her lover for attempting to leave her. Her crime immediately defines her as a woman beyond the law—but not as far as she first appears, because she inhabits a society with little respect for the law. The cynical, bored reporters and policemen are uninterested in what has happened until her frank admission of guilt. This confession propels people to her defense—not out of concern for her or her plight, but to advance their reputations, increase their salaries, or both. "Here I've just been prayin' for a nice, juicy murder," Jake Callahan the reporter says initially. "For two weeks now we haven't had nothin' but machine guns and hijackers" (15). Elated over the "sweet story" in this particular crime, he debates which approach will best realize its potential. "I'm callin' you 'the most beautiful murderess'" (14), he first announces. Upon reflection, he decides, "This one's got the makin's: wine, woman, jazz, a lover" (16). Finally, he concludes that the focus of his account should be "she kills him rather than lose him" (17). Jake's quest for the best "reading" assumes an array of possibilities with the determinant being not accuracy or justice but reader appeal.

Roxie's attorney Billy Flynn, on the other hand, is anxious that the accounts of her bolster his defense. Equally oblivious to justice, he is only concerned about his five-thousand-dollar fee, which he raises at the outset of his first meeting with Roxie. That settled, his first advice is to "go out for sympathy through the press" (41). Shrewdly aware of newspapers' preoccupation with stories, he has his secretary prepare a press release, with Roxie as the designated author, which characterizes her life as proceeding "From Convent to Jail" (41), thereby transforming her angry, vengeful murder into a woeful case of a good girl gone wrong. Billy also encourages Roxie to cooperate with Mary Sunshine, who writes for Jake's competitor. Explaining how "only a woman can understand" (43), he realizes that Mary's sentimental fixation with the hardships of women will cause her reports on the horrors of Roxie's life to upstage her crime and aid his transformation of her confession into an effective defense. Thus, by the trial of the third act, Roxie has a new identity that exonerates her actions and makes her socially acceptable.

Much of the humor of this conspiratorial perversion of truth and justice comes from the play's operative assumption that everyone, especially the audience, prefers Roxie's fabricated image and absurd explanation to the hard evidence of her lover's corpse. Her radical transformation from vengeful killer into a tearful victim of misfortune and exemplar of demure femininity wins her acquittal. Her willingness to be reconfigured into this tabloid Cinderella feeds the city's voracious appetite for diversions and earns her celebrity, exoneration, and a career in show business.

Chicago is not just a witty portrait of how grievous crimes get converted into personal gain; the comedy was itself deeply involved in this process. One small but telling example of this was the play's promotional strategy that offered its comic view of crime as a triumph of urban sophistication over provincial morality. During its pre-opening run in New Haven, New York newspapers carried a seemingly negative report of how John Archer, a professor from Yale's Divinity School, had stomped out and demanded that local police close the show. Archer was quoted as saying: "The satirical comedy, 'Chicago,' which is now running at the Shubert Theatre, seems to me entirely too vile for public performance. . . . Why flaunt that sort of life within the realm of drama? Why not leave the lid on the sewer and keep the stench from the nostrils of our Eastern public?"[6] Archer was incensed that Watkins was getting audiences to laugh at the kind of corruption that was producing gangland slayings, but it is hard to read these notices without suspecting that Sam Harris, *Chicago's* wily, veteran producer, was responsible for them.[7] He would have realized that audiences in New York gravitated more toward the outlook of the *American Mercury* and H. L. Mencken's assault upon "the New Puritanism" in the outlying area. Likewise, he would have sensed their identification with the self-congratulatory sophistication of the even newer *New Yorker* and its bold claim to *not* being for "the little old lady from Dubuque."

In short, Harris was hoping that New Yorkers would consider this divinity professor an exemplar of narrow-minded provinciality and Watkins's play solid proof of Chicago's cultural inferiority. And he succeeded. In a typical comment from the original reviews, Watkins was described as "excellently suited to tell the world all it need know about the city of Chicago": in praising her achievement, another reviewer claimed that *Chicago* ought to become "so monstrously and so conspicuously a hit that a flustered Chamber of Commerce in Chicago will either ban it from their city or else take steps to rectify some of the conditions."[8] "What the author has tried to do," wrote George Jean Nathan, the dean of New York drama critics, "is to set forth a caricature of the Illinois frontier town that hides behind a mask of metropolitan civilization."[9]

This opportunistic exploitation of New York biases spilled over into the publicity about the unknown author of *Chicago* and created an enormous misunderstanding of how she came to write her comedy. A profile of Watkins, which appeared in the *New York Times* just following the successful debut of her play, opened: "A rough surmise as to what sort of young woman wrote *"Chicago"* would probably lead to the conclusion that it was a person who is the diametric opposite of Maurine Watkins."[10] Like the other profiles of Watkins that appeared in New York newspapers, this one portrayed her rural midwestern upbringing and education as a formidable obstacle to her achievement. In a strained attempt at informality, the author displays amazement that anyone from such deprivation could ever have written sophisticated comedy: "a trusted scout, still grimy as a result of train rides through the Middle West, reports that in what used to be known as a girl's adolescence she could have been found in the vicinity of Crawsfordsville, Indiana."[11]

Watkins's later relocation to the East is presented as the missing link between this background and her accomplishment. Like the other profiles, this one would spotlight Watkins's enrollment in George Pierce Baker's English 47 at the newly opened Yale School of Drama and her reception of the highest grade ever awarded by this renowned teacher of American playwrights.[12] The account's somewhat unusual notation of the two years Watkins spent at Radcliffe pursing a Ph.D. in classics lent additional support to this explanation for her unlikely play.[13]

These biases erupt full-blown in the article's concluding assertion that "what the Chicago Chamber of Commerce has to say (about Watkins's play) won't count." This sweeping dismissal is important not so much for its condescension toward Chicago as its gross misrepresentation of Watkins's experience there:

> The high light of her newspaper experience—and the high light, for that matter, of several Chicago reporters' newspaper experience—was the Leopold-Loeb case, which she covered and about which she wrote feature stories concerning the psychological angle . . . it was the experience of reporting the Leopold-Loeb case that supplied her with much of the material for 'Chicago.'[14]

This linkage of Watkins with the so-called crime of the century must have seemed odd since its implications were so much more serious and troubling than Roxie's murder. While the intense newspaper interest in this trial *might* have inspired Watkins's thinking about Roxie's, it, in fact, did not. Much of what happens in her play and a large measure of its clever humor came straight out of a quite different assignment that Watkins covered during her year of work for the *Chicago Tribune*. She and Harris were probably responsible for the suppression of this assignment and probably did so to promote a belief that her comedy was inspired by contact with the East. However, Watkins also had very personal reasons for hiding this assignment. At the time, she worried over how audiences might respond to her play were they to know how deeply she herself was involved in the process she was mocking.[15] Her later reluctance to release the rights to her play stemmed from this worry's evolution into a deep-seated guilt that her witty *Chicago Tribune* articles had been responsible for murderesses going free.[16]

On March 12, 1924, two Cook County policemen found the body of Walter Law slumped over the steering wheel of an automobile owned by Mrs. Belva Gaertner, a cabaret singer with a long history of affairs. Initially, she denied responsibility for the shooting, but when confronted with the fact that the murder weapon was hers, lamely replied, "I don't know. I was drunk."[17] As a fledgling reporter for the *Chicago Tribune*, Watkins was assigned the lowly job of covering police reports and was on duty as the case unfolded. Already wise enough to know that a conventional report of this all-too-familiar crime would be buried in her newspaper's back pages, she decided to cover the case as an important event and to spice it up with flashes of wry humor.

Belva Gaertner, in jail just following her arrest for killing Walter Law. *Chicago Tribune* photo.

Not only did this approach get her first two reports featured, but it also secured her an exclusive interview with Gaertner and permission to cover the entire case. Sensing that Belva was guilty of premeditated murder, she recognized that her comments possessed an outspoken candor that was refreshing, funny, and, above all, good copy. Dutifully, she reported Belva's ingenuous observation: "Gin and guns—either one is bad enough, but together they get you in a dickens of a mess." Young, unmarried, and well-aware of the power and privilege men enjoyed, Watkins appreciated the comic aptness of Gaertner's quirky reflection: "I liked him and he loved me—but no woman can love a man enough to kill him. They aren't worth it, because there are always plenty more." Under the tongue-in-cheek headline "No Sweetheart Worth Killing—Mrs. Gaertner," Watkins opened her report, "No sweetheart in the world is worth killing—especially when you've had a flock of them—and the world knows it" (Mar. 14).

Though neither a comic strip nor a tabloid, the *Chicago Tribune* understood the importance of humor and hyping the mundane to its newspaper's appeal. Consequently, it quickly recognized the entertainment value in Watkins's reports and treated them like valuable contributions. Her success at converting a murderess into a zany character who entertained readers spurred her to scrutinize the daily arrest records for more opportunities.

Less than a month later, on April 3, another married woman wound up in the Cook County jail for killing her lover, and this time Watkins landed her humorous report on the *Tribune's* front page. Beneath a headline proclaiming "Woman Plays Jazz Air as Victim Dies," Watkins wrote, "Mrs. Beulah Annan, a comely young wife, played a foxtrot record named 'Hula Lou.' . . . Then she telephoned her husband and reported that she had killed a man who 'tried to make love' to her." For Watkins, the "Hula Lou" was merely a hook to get her reader's attention; her real interest was Beulah's story. Having first told the police that she had shot Harry Kalstedt to save her honor, Beulah revealed to the Assistant State Attorney that she was actually quite receptive to his early morning visit and offer of drink. In this account, she explained how in jest she told Kalstedt that she wanted to end their affair. To her surprise and dismay, he agreed and prepared to leave. At this point, she shot him (Apr. 4).

Given the similarity of these two killings, readers must have thought it strange that Watkins's report on Beulah made no mention of Belva. Whether this was an oversight or the conscious decision of a budding professional, she came out two days later with one more humorous article that now bore her name in a byline[18]—this time on the grim kinship of her subjects and Beulah's resourceful adaptation to her new environment. Alongside a picture of the pair together and overhead caption "Killers of Men," her article reported that "as yet the two have not talked over their common interests. A man, a woman, liquor and a gun." Seeing them side by side and realizing that they were in the same jail, the reader wonders how they could *not* have talked about their "common interests." With this information called into question by the format, Watkins concentrates on the further evolution of Beulah's story. In contrast to her original statement to the police of how "my mind went in a whirl," which echoed Belva's mental lapse, this "prettiest murderess," as Watkins identified her, now claimed to have a vivid recollection of her actions. With her original confusion and fit of jealousy reformulated into a battle with Kalstedt over the murder weapon and deep remorse over the outcome, Beulah's confession was neatly differentiated from Belva's and shaded toward a defense. Watkins

Beulah Annan, the "prettiest murderess." Chicago Historical Society neg. DN-76, 798.

reinforced this interpretation with a casual notation that the well-known criminal attorney W. W. O'Brien would represent Beulah (Apr. 6). With her eye fixed on the contrivance of Beulah's remarks and her precocious understanding of jailhouse theater, Watkins adeptly exploited the humor of her changing story and did all she could to keep readers interested in Beulah.

That Beulah's story would go through additional permutations was to be expected, but even Watkins was surprised by her announcement that she was pregnant, one day after another inmate, an illiterate immigrant, was sentenced to life for killing her lover. But Watkins was not shocked enough to miss this opportunity for her wit. On Friday, May 9, below a headline announcing "Beulah Annan Awaits Stork, Murder Trial," Watkins asked:

> What counts with a jury when a woman is on trial for murder?
>
> Youth? Beauty? And if to these she adds approaching motherhood—?

Pursuing the question of "what affects a jury anyway?," she skillfully directed her reader's attention away from Beulah and her pregnancy to the defenses of her sister inmates. This review was accompanied by a rough assessment of each one's chances of escaping conviction (May 9).

By this point, Watkins had *Tribune* readers closely following "Murderess Row" and elevated the attractive Beulah Annan to celebrity status. Belva's lawyers shrewdly repositioned her trial to follow Beulah's.[19] The commencement of the Annan trial not only received front page coverage but rivaled the discovery of Bobby Franks's body (May 24). When the jury reached its decision the next day, the *Tribune* devised a special sub-headline to go just beneath the bold, edge-to-edge proclamation "All City Hunts Kidnapers" to announce "Jury Finds Beulah Annan is 'Not Guilty.'" Watkins's opening reference to the "'beauty-proof' jury" flourished a concern for the impact her articles might have had on the proceedings, but the remainder of her coverage concentrated on levity and festivity. With large pictures of Beulah posing with members of the jury, punctuated references to "the glare of motion picture lights," and blocks of testimony that reinforced this impression, Watkins's account captured the occasion's carnival spirit. Quoting the prosecutor's plea that the jury decide "whether you want to let another pretty woman go out and say, 'I got away with it!'" Watkins concluded, "And they did" (May 25).

Watkins's characterization of Belva as a jailhouse version of Pygmalion's statue for the opening of her trial ten days later confirmed that the grim mood of the Leopold-Loeb case had not squelched her sense of humor.

> "Class"—that was Belva. For she lived up to her reputation as "the most stylish" of murderess' row: a blue twill suit bound with black braid, and white lacy frill down the front; patent leather slippers with shimmering French heels, chiffon gun metal hose. And a hat—ah, that hat! helmet shaped, with a silver buckle and cockade of ribbon, with one streamer tied jauntily—coquettishly—bewitchingly—under her chin. (June 4)

Nevertheless, the relegation of this delightful characterization to page four suggested that the Franks murder was altering the climate for her murderesses and her reports. Watkins's account of Belva's acquittal still made the front page, but it was shorter, more mannered, and noticeably more restrained. Her follow-up account entitled "Murderess Row Loses Class as Belva Is Freed" offered a fond farewell to her colorful inmates.

Belva Gaertner at the time of her trial in the hat that helped to make her the "most stylish" of murderess' row. *Chicago Tribune* photo.

Whether or not Watkins was reassigned to the Leopold-Loeb trial,[20] it quickly became the only trial in the news. By year's end, she had lost interest in reporting, left the *Tribune*, and relocated to New York City. There, she accepted an editorial position to pay her bills and began commuting to Yale with hopes of converting her sprightly articles into stage comedy.

Watkins's experience in Chicago enabled her to understand that New Yorkers were not unique in their appreciation for the humor in crime. She also realized that their appreciation was not so adversely impacted by the Franks's slaying and the erupting gangland violence. Moreover, she was convinced that her prospects were increased by their ignorance of the events that so entertained the readers of her *Tribune* articles. As shrewd as this assessment proved to be, it benefited enormously from an event that did not even happen until after her play was completed.

One telling measure of *Chicago's* appeal to the New Yorkers who first saw it can be gleaned from the comments of a reviewer who urged his readers not to exempt themselves from its comic indictment:

> New York may laugh at it as a parody of Chicago, but just the same it is nationally applicable to the current tendency to turn a trial into a rousing free show rather than a sober quest for justice. In fact, local tabloids who have been growling at each other might well claim today that the play is an exposure of the other sheet's methods.[21]

This rather cryptic observation referenced a trial that attracted as much attention as that of Leopold and Loeb and one that started, quite fortuitously, just as *Chicago* was being readied for its Broadway opening. Over the summer of 1926, a four-year-old murder case came roaring back to life. On September

16, 1922, the bodies of Reverend Edward W. Hall and Mrs. Eleanor Mills, a married member of his church's choir, were discovered on a remote lovers' lane near Brunswick, New Jersey. Both had been shot, and their bodies had been carefully positioned to suggest romantic involvement. Around them were scattered fragments of their love letters. Clearly, the killer wanted their adulterous involvement exposed and avenged. Suspicion immediately focused upon the surviving spouses. After months of debate and speculation, preliminary charges were finally filed against Hall's wealthy, overweight wife, who was seven years his senior. But the grand jury judged the evidence insufficient and refused to indict her.[22]

By 1926, the case was a dusty, nearly forgotten file when a maid who had testified on Mrs. Hall's behalf was accused by her husband in a divorce proceeding of lying and receiving five thousand dollars in hush money. This questionable revelation would have had little impact had the *New York Mirror* not seized it and converted it into banner headlines. At the time, this two-year-old Hearst newspaper was straining to break the market dominance enjoyed by the *Daily News*, the first American tabloid (1919). Through featured, biased accounts of the case, the *Mirror* pushed for a trial and reader attention. By November, pressure was sufficiently intense that local officials approved charges against Mrs. Hall and her two brothers. The *Mirror* sparked enough interest that every New York paper felt compelled to cover the eighteen-day trial, which generated a staggering nine million words of print.[23] Damon Runyon, then a sportswriter for the *American*, was reassigned so that his accounts would be as colorful as his sports reports and would help his paper retain its readership.[24] Such attempts to wring high drama from the conflicting testimonies reached fever pitch when a self-proclaimed witness to the killing, nicknamed "the pig woman," was brought into the courtroom on a stretcher and encouraged to croak out her damning recollections. However, Mrs. Hall's defense proved stronger than the case against her. On December 3, less than four weeks before *Chicago* opened, Mrs. Hall, like Belva Gaertner, Beulah Annan, and Roxie Hart, was found not guilty.[25]

The Hall trial and the accompanying tidal wave of news coverage endowed the events of Watkins's play with a relevance that eliminated all need to explain or defend their meaning. To the extent that Watkins's experience with the *Tribune* educated her in the way the press was exploiting and altering the judicial process, her comedy was able to anticipate not just the Hall trial but the even bigger ones of today.

"They're awful dumb, reporters," observes the Matron of the jail in a keynote remark. "Never get anything right" (28). Her familiarity with the news reporters covering her jail make her knowledgeable on how facts regularly get distorted and changed. Her estimate that reporters are "dumb" is a naive explanation laced with irony and cued to Roxie's initial dismay at newspapers' inaccuracy and distortion of truth. As she subsequently reads about herself in them, Roxie senses the power of the press and takes a momentous first step in her growth and education. "Why, it's just like I was President or somethin'," she exclaims (25). At this point, Roxie does not understand the way newspapers eradicate social and moral distinctions, but she immediately grasps the elevated status being conferred upon her. As a photographer points out in getting her to pose for him, "You'll be right along with President Coolidge and Harold McCormick—there ain't a society dame in town but what would jump at the chance!" (18).

Before this lesson in the value of publicity can be converted into a release from jail, Roxie has to learn to "play ball," as

Watkins originally entitled her play. Reporters, like everyone else rallying around her, must be repaid for their support. For newspapers to continue their coverage, she needs to provide them interesting copy. This discovery leads to a realization that newspapers are simply one aspect of an entrenched urban conspiracy that demands that she be eye-catching if she is to get noticed. Along with pressuring her to be different or unusual, it insists that her conduct conform to established expectations. Roxie first notices that her jail contains other inmates who have killed their male companions for very similar reasons: abuse. The Matron even concedes that these murders were probably justified. "I never hear of a man's bein' killed but I know he got *just* what was comin' to him" (26), she remarks. Yet her hastily added qualification—"But you mustn't *say* it" (26)—informs Roxie of a crucial axiom of her education in image construction. However justified these women may have been, any claim that men deserved killing is not a valid defense or even an appropriate matter for discussion.

To be found innocent, these murderesses must disavow their original motives and ally themselves with the traditional expectation that women be attractive, loyal, and submissive. For her trial, the fashionable Velma develops a demeanor that matches her clothes. Her flourish of refinement and sensitivity seeks to convince the jury that she "wouldn't hurt a worm" (26). Her murderous retaliation against her husband for his divorce request is reworked into a story of willing acceptance that makes her appear compliant and dumb—an exemplary wife. Similarly, Liz's righteous anger is recast as madness, not for legal reasons so much as for its display of the daffiness and irresponsibility commonly associated with women. These transformations further Roxie's education and help her to understand the importance of dressing like the fairer sex and behaving like the weaker one. Soon she is feeding newspapers stories that reinforce this image. Meanwhile, her lawyer instructs her on how to get it into her court appearance. "Remember," he advises, "no matter what he [the prosecuting attorney] *says* or how mad he gets, you shrink—and cower—and cry . . . [act] weak, faint, frightened—always to the jury—with a little flutter" (80–81). In short: look like a conventional woman and not like the angry, assertive one who killed Casely when he threatened to leave.

The single most important element of this education, by far, is for Roxie to understand that appearance is critical and that actual reform is unnecessary and even undesirable. Roxie's counselors—Jake, Billy, and the Matron—flagrantly disregard and violate the advice they offer. They realize that dress and demeanor are merely *show*, necessary capitulation to a culture unwilling to relinquish what it no longer believes. In their counsel and conduct, these cunning, hard-bitten cynics encourage her to make rehabilitation an appearance and to cultivate it with the same determination, resourcefulness, and duplicity they deploy.

In the end, Roxie succeeds precisely because she alters *only* her appearance. The first act orients her toward the changes, while the second act shows her developing the necessary dissimulation. First, she steals Velma's dress from Marshall Field in order to appear more demure and feminine. Then, to get funds to pay Billy, she auctions it off as memorabilia of "the first time I ever went wrong" (60). Shaken when reporters abandon her repetitious tales of guilt for the fresher stories of new inmates, Roxie invents a pregnancy and transforms herself into a "deserted wife and mother" (76) to bring them back. Decidedly not the weak, submissive woman on display, Roxie channels her strength and determination into her performance and wins exoneration. Within this sham of capitulation to discredited values lurks a now liberated woman adept at manipulating her image and getting her way. Acquitted of her crime, she has truly become the assertive, determined woman of the opening scene. Appropriately, she brings down the final curtain with an announcement that she is leaving her husband and embarking on a career in show business.

Watkins's depiction of Roxie's indoctrination into the tabloid culture of her age made her comedy engaging not just to New Yorkers but to Chicagoans as well. When *Chicago* opened in Chicago in September of 1927, New Yorkers watched to see if it would offend the locals and affirm their conjectures.[26] To their chagrin, it was just as successful, though for quite different reasons. Stung by New York's haughty references to their city, Chicago residents went out of their way to show themselves equally capable of enjoying good comedy. "It were silly for the most devoted of us as Chicagoans to be resentful because the piece is called '*Chicago*,'" wrote the reviewer for Watkins's former employer, the *Chicago Tribune*; "that is, after all, the best title for it. And I hope the play is so much of a success here that it will run and run."[27] Along with this refutation went a determination to turn the play into a celebration. In contrast to New York where the play's origins were suppressed, Chicagoans were encouraged to recall the people and entertaining articles that had inspired it. Belva came to the opening dressed to kill. In an article for the *Chicago Herald Examiner* entitled "Belva Sees *Chicago* and Relives Killing," Cook County's most stylish murderess referenced Velma and proclaimed, "Sure, that's me." "Roxie Hart's supposed to be Beulah Annan," she went on to explain. "She was the most beautiful woman ever accused of murder."[28] Another article in the *Chicago Post*, with an accompanying picture of W. W. O'Brien alongside Watkins and Francine Larrimore who played Roxie, observed that several of Billy Flynn's lines came straight from his defense of Beulah. "O'Brien accepted the play upon its face value," it observed, "stating that, in his opinion, it is the finest piece of stage satire ever written by an American."[29] What it did not explain was O'Brien's hope that this would resurrect a brighter moment of his career and dispel the adverse publicity of his wounding when he was with Hymie Weiss at his slaying on the steps of Holy Name Cathedral.[30] Mayor William Hale Thompson was thinking along similar lines when he proposed that Watkins be made publicity agent for the city of Chicago and, wryly recycling the comments of the *Daily Telegraph's* review and the *New York Times* profile, characterized her as "excellently suited to tell the world all it need know about the city of Chicago."[31] Very conscious of how the worsening gangland feuds were blackening the public's perception of Chicago, O'Brien, and many others in the audience, responded to *Chicago* as a nostalgic journey back to happier times when the killers in the headlines were women and the depiction of them could be light-hearted.

If *Chicago* actually profited from this darkening of the cultural climate, it proved fatal for Watkins. The Leopold-Loeb trial had already shown how the market for her skills could turn, but this point was driven home even more forcefully before the disappointing opening of *Revelry*, her melodrama about the corruptions of the Harding administration, and her lost years in Hollywood. Ironically, the success of *Chicago* created more demand for her as journalist than playwright. New York newspapers eagerly recruited her to cover trials involving women. First, the *World* commissioned her to comment on the heavily covered divorce case between "Peaches" and "Daddy" Browning.[32] Next, the *Daily Telegraph* offered her a handsome fee to cover the trial of Ruth Snyder and Judd Gray for the crime of murdering her husband so they might marry and collect a forty-eight-thousand-dollar insurance policy with a double indemnity clause.[33] Here was another murder trial involving a murderess who was hoping that a radical make-over might win her exoneration. However, there was nothing humorous about the sordid details of this pair's relationship and the calloused ineptitude of their murder. Both were convicted and sentenced to the electric chair. A picture of Snyder's execution, which breached security, was published on the front page of the *Daily News* and overnight became the most famous photograph of the decade. Confronted with material that James Cain would shape into memorable novels, Watkins was out of her element—this time for good. Never again would she find material that matched her talents as the trials of Belva and Beulah had.

On the other hand, the fascination with crime, celebrity, and image fabrication, which factored so prominently into the background and writing of *Chicago*, has only intensified and increased the pertinence of her comedy. These were significant considerations in the 1940 decision to make *Roxie Hart*. They were very much on the minds of the producers who sought the rights to Watkins's play back in the 1950s and 1960s. Indeed, they factored prominently into the enthusiastic reception of the Fosse musical when it finally opened in 1975. Today, they are more evident than ever. As criticisms mount over the way newspapers, the nightly television news, and prime-time gossip shows exploit trials to hold their audience's attention, *Chicago* reminds us that the 1920s had its own Amy's and O.J.'s. Indeed, it portrays a culture enough like our own that it deserves to be remembered.

NOTES

1. Burns Mantle, ed., *The Best Plays of 1926–27* (New York: Dodd, Mead, 1927), 452. *Chicago* played successfully in Detroit, Boston, Los Angeles, and Chicago. The film version, a DeMille production, was released in February 1928.

2. According to her Radcliffe application, Watkins was born on July 27, 1896. By the time she applied to the Yale School of Drama, she had already moved her birth date back to 1898 and thereafter regularly led people to believe that she was younger than she actually was. At the time *Chicago* opened, several articles gave her age as twenty-six, though she was in fact thirty. Living in an age that accorded young people unprecedented esteem and working in a field with restricted female participation, Watkins was eager to associate herself with the new spirit of youth and change.

3. By the time of her death, Watkins was so forgotten that the *New York Times* did not offer an obituary notice.

4. Maurine Watkins, *Chicago* (New York: Knopf, 1927). Burns Mantle also included it among the ten plays gathered in *The Best Plays of 1926–27*. Subsequent references to *Chicago* will be included parenthetically in the text.

5. Back in the early 1950s, Robert Fryer, one of the producers of the 1975 musical, laid plans for a musical version of *Chicago*. These plans called for the role of Roxie to go to Gwen Verdon who later got Fosse interested in the property and wound up playing Roxie in the 1975 production. But Fryer's original plans were torpedoed by Watkins's refusal to sell the necessary rights. Already an eccentric recluse and born-again Christian, Watkins would have nothing to do with either Fryer or several other producers with similar plans. She even paid Robert Rumsey of the American Play Company to keep such people from bothering her. When Sheldon Abend succeeded Rumsey, he mounted a careful campaign to persuade Watkins to relinquish the rights to *Chicago*. Though she entertained his offers and expressed a willingness, she always balked at signing the necessary papers. This reluctance prevented Abend from securing the rights until after her death. Newspaper clipping misidentified as *New York Times*, Jan. 29, 1973, *Chicago* clipping files, Katherine Cornell Library for the Performing Arts at Lincoln Center (hereafter identified as KCL-LC). *New York Times*, July 28, 1974, 24. Sheldon Abend, telephone conversation with editor, May 17, 1993. Kevin Boyd Grubb, *Razzle Dazzle: The Life and Work of Bob Fosse* (New York: St. Martin's Press, 1989), 193.

6. *New York Times*, Dec. 28, 1926, 21. In a follow-up story the next day, Archer was quoted as calling the play "vile, immoral, blasphemous, and a storm of nastiness." *New York Times*, Dec. 29, 1926, 10.

7. In his influential analysis of the press during the twenties, Silas Bent examined the powerful influence of publicity agents and estimated that somewhere between 40 and 60 percent of the information in newspapers was provided by these agents. Silas Bent, *Ballyhoo: The Voice of the Press* (New York: Boni and Liveright, 1927), 122–23. At the time, Harris employed a full-time press representative to handle situations like this, so it was probably Alex Yokel, rather than Harris, who circulated this story.

8. *New York Daily Telegraph*, Jan. 1, 1927 and New York Daily Telegram, Dec. 31, 1926. KCL-LC.

9. *American Mercury* 10 (Mar. 1927): 376. Nathan's review, slightly enlarged, was presented as an introduction to the published version of the play.

10. "The Author of 'Chicago,'" *New York Times*, Jan. 2, 1927, sec. 7, 1.

11. "The Author of 'Chicago,'" *New York Times*, Jan. 2, 1927, sec. 7, 1. This "trusted scout" apparently had as little to do with the Midwest as possible since the report that Watkins attended and graduated from Wabash College was incorrect. She attended Hamilton College and Transylvania College—both in Lexington, Kentucky—before transferring to Butler College, from which she graduated a year and a half later in 1919.

12. Brooks Atkinson even cited this information in his review of the play. *New York Times*, Dec. 31, 1926, 11.

13. If this information helped to make this the most thorough profile, it nonetheless failed to mention that Watkins actually enrolled in Baker's English 47 twice while he was still there. Her Radcliffe transcript shows that she took English 47 during the 1919–20 academic year and then again during the 1920–21 year. On her transcript, her repeat is described as "open only to those who have taken English 47 with distinction."

14. "The Author of 'Chicago,'" *New York Times*, Jan. 2, 1927, sec. 7, 1.

15. Brooks Atkinson's characterization of Watkins's play in his review illustrates the broad-based aversion toward the aggressive commercialization of crime that was occurring: "*Chicago* is not a melodrama, as the prologue indicates, but a satirical comedy on the administration of justice through the fetid channels of newspaper publicity—of photographers, 'sob sisters,' feature stunts, standardized prevarication and generalized vulgarity." *New York Times*, Dec. 31, 1926, 11.

16. Sheldon Abend, telephone conversation with the editor, May 17, 1993.

17. *Chicago Tribune*, March 12, 1924, 1. All future references to Watkins's *Chicago Tribune* articles are cited by date in the text of the Introduction. These articles can be found in this volume following the text of Watkins's play.

18. Watkins actually received her first byline identification on her article the day before—April 5, 1924.

19. Belva's trial was originally scheduled for April 21, 1924. *Chicago Tribune*, March 28, 1924, 16.

20. In an article entitled "Front Page Drama or Stage Tales of Two Cities" for *Liberty Magazine*, April 23, 1927, Burns Mantle reported that Watkins "was not assigned to the Leopold-Loeb case as is so often reported." (54) KCL-LC.

21. *New York Telegram*, Dec. 31, 1926. The review of *Chicago*, which appeared in the *New York Daily Telegraph*, Jan. 1927, supported this estimate in its characterization of the comedy as biting "the yellow hand of modern journalism, a cult whose St. Peter was William Randolph Hearst and whose Martin Luther was Bernard Macfadden." KCL-LC.

22. William M. Kunstler, *The Hall-Mills Murder Case: The Minister and the Choir Singer* (New Brunswick: Rutgers Univ. Press, 1964), 4–7, 102.

23. Kunstler, 115–18. John Mosedale, *The Men Who Invented Broadway: Damon Runyon, Walter Winchell, and Their World* (New York: Richard Marek, 1981), 137–42. *This Fabulous Century 1920–1930*, vol. 3 (New York: Time-Life, 1969), 190. Though Kunstler acknowledges this media pressure, he concentrates much more on the trial itself and the question of what really happened. Mosedale is much better on this very important context.

24. Mosedale, 137–42.

25. Following this verdict, the Hall family filed a defamation case against the *Mirror*. The $150,000 that it originally sought was much publicized, but the sum actually agreed upon was never disclosed. Kunstler, 309.

26. At least two New York newspapers offered articles summarizing what the Chicago reviewers wrote about Watkins's comedy. See *New York Daily News*, Sept. 13, 1927 and *World*, Sept. 25, 1927. KCL-LC.

27. *Chicago Tribune*, Sept. 12, 1927. KCL-LC.

28. *Chicago Herald Examiner*, Sept. 19, 1927. KCL-LC. Beulah did not attend because, a few months before, she had married a garage owner and relocated to Crown Point, Indiana. There she learned that her third husband was still married. After filing for a divorce, she suffered a mental breakdown and died a year later at a mental hospital where she was registered under an assumed name.

29. *Chicago Post*, Sept. 12, 1927. KCL-LC.

30. Laurence Bergreen, *Capone: The Man and the Era* (New York: Simon and Schuster, 1994), 208.

31. *New York Telegraph*, Apr. 8, 1927. Also *Daily Star*, Apr. 9, 1927. KCL-LC.

32. Maurine Watkins, "Our Peaches Has Got to Have a Jury!," *World*, Metropolitan Sec. 1, 8.

33. Between April 18 and May 7, 1927, Watkins wrote seventeen articles for the *New York Telegram*. In the opening paragraph of his *Ballyhoo* (1927), Silas Bent asserted, "On any basis of authentic valuation the sinking of the Titanic was a bigger story than the Snyder-Gray murder trial" in order to accent how it nonetheless was given a bigger "play" (21). Watkins was one of an estimated 120 reporters to cover it.

Cast List from the Original Production of *Chicago*

CHICAGO

(172 performances)

Satirical comedy in three acts by Maurine Watkins. Produced by Sam H. Harris at the Music Box Theatre, New York, December 30, 1926.

Cast of characters—

Roxie Hart . . . . Francine Larrimore
Fred Casely . . . . Doan Borup
Jake . . . . Charles A. Bickford
Amos Hart . . . . Charles Halton
Sergeant Murdock . . . . Charles Slattery
Martin S. Harrison . . . . Robert Barrat
Babe . . . . Arthur R. Vinton
Slats . . . . G. Albert Smith
Mrs. Morton . . . . Isabelle Winlocke
Velma . . . . Juliette Crosby
Liz . . . . Dorothy Stickney
Billy Flynn . . . . Edward Ellis
Mary Sunshine . . . . Eda Heineman
Moonshine Maggie . . . . Ferike Boros
Go-To-Hell Kitty . . . . Edith Fitzgerald
Bailiffs . . . . Carl De Mal, George Lanning
Judge Canton . . . . Milano Tilden
Woman Reporter . . . . Wilma Thompson
First Man Reporter . . . . George Cowell
Clerk of the Court . . . . Charles Kuhn
First Photographer . . . . James C. Pall
Stenographer . . . . Vincent York
Foreman of the Jury . . . . G. W. Anspake
Cameramen . . . . Thomas Poland, Al Milliken
    Act I.—Roxie's Bedroom. South Side, Chicago.
    Act II.—Women's Ward, Cook County Jail.
    Act III.—Prisoners' Room in Criminal Court Building and Judge
        Canton's Court.
    Staged by George Abbott

CHICAGO

CHARACTERS

ROXIE HART, *"the prettiest woman ever charged with murder in Chicago."*
FRED CASELY, *"the other man."*
AMOS HART, *"her meal-ticket husband."*
BILLY FLYNN, *her attorney—"best in the city, next to Halliday."*
MARTIN S. HARRISON, *Assistant State's Attorney.*
CHARLES E. MURDOCK, *police sergeant.*
JAKE, *reporter on The Morning Gazette.*
BABE, *photographer on The Morning Gazette.*
MARY SUNSHINE, *sob sister on The Evening Star.*
MRS. MORTON, *matron at Cook County Jail.*
VELMA, *"stylish divorcée."* ⎤
LIZ, *"God's Messenger."* ⎟ *Inmates*
MOONSHINE MAGGIE, *"hunyak."* ⎬ *of*
GO-TO-HELL KITTY, *"the Tiger Girl."* ⎟ *Murderess*
MACHINE-GUN ROSIE, *the Cicero Kid.* ⎦ *Row*
Judge, Jury, Bailiffs, Clerk, Photographers, Reporters.

PROLOGUE, Friday night. Bedroom of Amos Hart.
ACT I, Sunday afternoon—two days later. Woman's Ward of the Cook County Jail.
ACT II, noon one month later. Same as Act I.
ACT III:
SCENE 1, morning—seven weeks later. Prisoner's room.
SCENE 2, later—same day. Judge Canton's Court.

CHICAGO—PRESENT DAY

PROLOGUE

PROLOGUE

Six fifty-eight P. M., April the third.
SCENE: *Bedroom of* AMOS HART *and others. A corner room, first floor, in one of those cheap modern flats on Chicago's South Side. There's an entrance with fountain and flowers, but pine and beaver-board within. Mission finish to the heavily pretentious woodwork—solid doors, beams, and molding. Furniture red and glistening like a courtesan's polished nails. Flowered paper, gaudy rugs on the wide-board floor. Everything new and tawdry, everything cheap and shiny.*

Two windows [center rear] look out on the court, a door [left] opens into an adjoining room, and another [right] into a narrow hall, with living-room straight ahead and outside door [unseen]. Another door [left] opens into a small closet, filled ninety-eight per cent with feminine garments; two pairs of trousers and a coat are accorded one hook in the corner.

Between the two windows, with foot-board to the front, is a large brass bed, with covers thrown back in confusion and pillows tossed together. At its head is a night-table, with telephone, a stoutish bottle and a couple of glasses—empty but not unsoiled—an ashtray, and a box of cigarettes.

At the right is a large vanity-dresser, equipped with all the known weapons of offense and instruments of

3

preservation: bottles and atomizers, jars of cream, powder, rouge, perfumes—especially perfumes, that fill the air with their heavy cloying odors!—silver embossed brushes and comb filled with hair; manicure set of imitation ivory; eyebrow pencils, and lipstick. And over it all a heavy film of pinkish powder. Half-closed drawers reveal shoes, intimate garments—peach and pink crepe de chine with deep Val lace—soiled hose, hats, and gloves, in endless confusion.

To the left of the center window—between it and the door to the hall—is a victrola. There are records on the floor, sorted to the player's choice. It is playing now: heavy, rhythmic jazz, with the sinful insistence of the tom-tom and the saxophone's wailing plea.

The man, a man perhaps of thirty, stands in the doorway, pulling on his coat and turned to go. The woman, a girl of twenty-three or so, stands by the foot of the bed watching him, and she steadies herself with one hand on the rail. Steadies herself from emotion perhaps, perhaps from the drink that left empty bottle.

She is slender, beautifully slender; as you can see, through the diaphanous, flashy négligée of blue georgette with its flounce of imitation lace and accordion-plaited ruffles. And the face is beautiful, too, with short upper lip, pouting mouth, tiptilted nose, wide dark eyes, skin of the finest texture, and hair the color of flame. Turned now in profile there's a hint of a Raphael angel—with a touch of Medusa.

ROXIE [*a shrill, hysterical voice that is vile in anger*]:
You damned tightwad!
[*Her voice is lowered with hatred.*]

Like *hell* you're through!

[*One white arm flings around to the dresser, one white hand searches the drawer and brings forth the latest necessity of milady's boudoir: a pearl-handled .32 revolver. Her voice stabs with virulent rage.*]

You God-damned *louse*—!

[*She pulls the trigger, then stands fixed: he sways, crumples, falls—a soft, thuddy fall. Outside the window children are singing and playing under the swaying arc-light; but within there is a silence. Except for the tom-tom's sensuous beat and the saxophone's last sad wail. From the next room comes the cheerful, idiotic call of the cuckoo: "Cuckoo . . . cuckoo . . . cuckoo . . ."* It's seven o'clock.*]

[*The curtain falls for an instant to denote the passage of three and one-half hours and it rises again on the same room, with the dead man removed. The table has been drawn out, and behind it sits* POLICE SERGEANT MURDOCK, *a heavy, bluff fellow of fifty or so, with ruddy face and heavy jowls. In the middle of the floor sits* AMOS, *an awkward creature of thirty-five or six, with a low forehead, snub nose, and a weak chin. He wears a noble, melancholy air, and enjoys the procedure thoroughly. His clothes bear the odor of the "shop," and his hands are marked with grease and grime.*]

[*A* NEWSPAPERMAN—*a rough and ready chap in the middle twenties, with keen eyes and cynical smile—leans over the foot of the bed, listening as the* SERGEANT *dictates to* AMOS, *who writes laboriously.*]

SERGEANT [*dictating*]: "Voluntarily and of my own free will——"

AMOS: Freely and gladly!

JAKE: Ain't he the cheerful murderer though!

AMOS [*quickly*]: That ain't murder—shootin' a burglar. Why, only last week the jury *thanked* a man!

JAKE [*scoffing*]: Burglar, huh!

AMOS [*excitedly*]: Well, he was! Climbin' right in that there window!

SERGEANT [*impatiently*]: Come on—*sign*.

AMOS: I ain't signin' nothin' 'ness he says it's a burglar.

SERGEANT: Say, he ain't tryin' the case—*sign*.

> [AMOS *signs;* OFFICER *takes and reads with satisfaction.*]

And mind yuh don't say we beat yuh up or showed yuh the goldfish or nothin' when yuh get on the witness-stand.

AMOS [*with injured dignity*]: I'll not. I gave myself up, you know. [*Dramatically.*] Surrendered myself to the law!

SERGEANT [*turns to* REPORTER, *who has taken the telephone*]: That wipes *that* off the books—God, how I hate to have 'em hangin' over "unsolved"! How's that for quick work, Gazette? [*He looks at his watch.*] The call come at 9:30, and in less than an hour we've made the arrest and got a signed confession!

JAKE [*at phone*]: Dearborn O-five hundred . . . right. . . . [*To the* SERGEANT.] Slick enough, all right! [*At the phone.*] City desk. . . .

SERGEANT: Put that in your story and don't forget who done it: Sergeant Charles E. Murdock—and *don't* forget the *E*.

JAKE: You know me!

SERGEANT [*with a grunt*]: I know your whole damn tribe!

JAKE [*at phone*]: Hello, Tommy, is the Boss there? . . . Well, gimme a rewrite man. . . . Callahan talking. [*In an easy, drawling monotone.*] Still on the Hart case . . . yeah, Coroner's just gone with the body—sure, he's dead, all right . . . Caseley's the name: C-A-S-E-L-Y. Found a card in his pocket —auto salesman for Waverly, 1861 South Michigan——

AMOS [*starts up*]: What's that? Didn't show *me* no card!

SERGEANT: Shut up.

JAKE [*in the phone*]: Might check on that—maybe there's a story *there*. Pretty tame here if he's tellin' the truth, but it sounds kinda' fishy to *me*. . . . Hart works at night, yuh see, mechanic at Phillips' Garage, 6701 Cottage Grove. . . . O, a queer cuss with an Andy Gump head on an Abe Lincoln chassis. . . . Well, he gets home a little after nine, finds his wife asleep, gets a snack to eat, comes back to the bedroom and finds this guy climbin' in the window, grabs his gun and lets him have it. . . . Yeah, they got a confession all right—came right across with it. . . . Sure, either crazy or knows his Chicago!

AMOS [*complacently*]: I ain't as dumb as I look.

SERGEANT: Hey, WHO got a confession?

JAKE: O yeah, Dicky, get this right now: the call was answered by Sergeant Charles E. Murdock— D-O-C-K—and Policeman— What's his name, Sergeant?—the gink outside?

SERGEANT: Patterson—Michael Patterson.

JAKE: —Patterson of the Hyde Park station, who made the arrest and obtained a signed confession in less than an hour. . . . And Martin S. Harrison is here from the State's Attorney's office—he's talkin' to the wife. And O baby, she's a red-hot mama with an angel face! We'll run her in the picture. . . .

AMOS: *Picture?*

JAKE: You've got the idee, but yuh better run it as straight news till I get more.dope; tame if true, and cheap any way yuh take it. . . . Sure, I'll ring yuh back when Babe gets here. . . . Right! . . . S'long. . . . [*Hangs up receiver and turns to* MUR-DOCK.] Say, Big Boy, the photographer's on his way —be here any minute now—for a couple of flashes. We can stick around till he gets here, huh?

SERGEANT: You newspaper fellahs think the whole police department is a show run for your benefit.

JAKE [*grinning*]: Well, ain't it?

SERGEANT: No, it *ain't*. I'm clearin' up this here case because it's in my line uh duty——

JAKE: Sure—it means your bread and butter. [*Slaps officer's knee.*] But don't forget where the jam comes from, Old Timer. You're one of our men, ain't yuh? Well, yuh've got to play ball.

SERGEANT: I am, ain't I? What do you want? See anyone here from the other papers? [*Chuckling.*] They're holdin' the bag at the station!

[ASSISTANT STATE'S ATTORNEY HARRISON *comes in from the next room. He is a tall young man of the student type, with eager, nervous manner— now almost bursting with suppressed excitement; a little near-sighted, with tortoise-shell glasses; aquiline nose, thin lips.*]

Well—well: I've *got* him for you, Mr. Assistant State's Attorney! And here's your confession, all sewed up!

HARRISON: Good!

SERGEANT [*cheerfully*]: Not that it amounts to a damn, for he'll deny every word of it when he comes to trial.

AMOS [*with dignity*]: I won't. I shot him, and I'm prepared——

JAKE: To wear a hero's medal!

HARRISON [*takes a seat facing* AMOS *and nods encouragingly*]: That's the way to talk now, and if you stick *to* it, I'll help you. Provided you make a clean breast of it.

SERGEANT: What's the matter? Tryin' to shoot holes in that confession? It's all there, ain't it, in black and white, and he tells just how he done it.

HARRISON: That clears your books, but *I* want to know the motive. [*Smiles pleasantly at* AMOS.] For you don't *look* like a man, Mr. Hart, who'd shoot a fellow-being down in cold blood.

AMOS: I didn't—I was defendin' my home, just like I told you: found him climbin' in the window——

HARRISON: A total stranger?

AMOS [*emphatically*]: Never saw him before in my life!

SERGEANT: My God, Harrison, *I* covered all that!

HARRISON [*ignoring* SERGEANT]: And your wife—are you willing to swear that he was a total stranger to her, too?

AMOS: Yes, sir.

HARRISON: All right; suppose you add that. [*Dictates, and* AMOS *scrawls in the stenographer's notebook.*] "To the best of my knowledge the deceased was also totally unknown to my wife, Roxie Hart."

AMOS [*signs statement*]: Say, what's the big idea?

HARRISON: I trust *you*, Mr. Hart, but not the attorney

you'll see tomorrow. [*He turns to others with satisfaction.*] They can't spring the "unwritten law" *now.*

AMOS: Say, there's no unwritten law in this!

HARRISON: I'll say there isn't! You've sworn it away right here! [*He opens the door and shoves* AMOS *into the charge of the* POLICEMAN *in the next room.*] Patterson! [*To the* SERGEANT.] Stranger, hell! Why, she's been carrying on with that guy for months! And admits it here [*he taps paper in his pocket*] in the nastiest little statements any jury ever read! [*He calls at door at left.*] MRS. HART! [*To the* SERGEANT] She's talking now, all right! [*Goes to room at right, with* AMOS, *and* ROXIE *enters: dishevelled, excited, with a look of furtive cunning in her eyes, red from weeping.*]

ROXIE: Where's my husband?

SERGEANT [*with a glance at her filmy costume*]: Say, you'd better get into some clothes, sister.

ROXIE: What for? *He* promised I'd go free—*I* ain't done nothin'.

SERGEANT [*shakes his head*]: Shake a leg, kid: clothes. [*She goes to the closet and begins dressing; no one minds, especially* ROXIE.] Well, well, so yuh been cheatin'! Ain't yuh 'shamed now, your sweetie dead and your husband held for murder? So you was right here all the time! And what did *you* do while he filled him full of lead, huh?

ROXIE [*with a little gasp of fear*]: Begged 'em to stop —fightin' they was; threw myself between 'em——

JAKE: The story picks up!

SERGEANT: *Fightin'?*

ROXIE [*gaining confidence*]: Sure—jealous! You should uh seen 'em—mad about me, both of 'em, *perfectly mad.* . . .

SERGEANT: Where d'yuh meet him?

ROXIE: At the office—where I work.

SERGEANT [*to* JAKE]: See? That's what happens when a woman leaves the home. [*To* ROXIE.] What do yuh do?

ROXIE: I'm a secretary.

SERGEANT: So you're a stenographer . . . humph. . . . [*Looking at statement.*] How long has this been goin' on? [*Pause.*] All right—speak up.

ROXIE: The first time—really—was Christmas.

SERGEANT: That's a nice way for a married woman to be carryin' on, now ain't it! . . . Plannin' to run off and marry him?

ROXIE [*genuinely surprised*]: *Marry* him? Hell, no!

JAKE: Just a good time on the side, with Goofy in there for a meal-ticket.

ROXIE: Meal-ticket! Say, he couldn't buy my liquor!

SERGEANT: Did this guy know you was married or was you foolin' him, too?

ROXIE [*comes out of closet in a poppy-colored dress and goes to dresser for make-up*]: So was he—a wife and kid!

[*Door at right opens:* AMOS *flings in, wild-eyed, with* HARRISON *following him.*]

HARRISON [*exultant*]: All right, here we are; we've got it at last, Mrs. Hart!

ROXIE [*flings herself about*]: *What?*

AMOS [*in a thick voice*]: So yuh been stringin' me!

HARRISON [*grabs* ROXIE'S *arm*]: *Why* did you kill him?

ROXIE [*gives a frightened glance around, considers*

a dash]: It's a lie! I didn't! Damn you, let go!
    [*She sinks her teeth in his wrist—he flings her
    off with an oath, and she sinks into a chair in hys-
    terical rage.*]
You said you'd stick, you said you'd——
AMOS: Sure, if he's a burglar! What d'yuh lie to me
    for?
ROXIE [*grinds out through her teeth*]: God damn you!
SERGEANT: So it was *you*.
ROXIE [*rises, hysterical*]: Yes, it was me! I shot him
    and I'm damned glad I did! I'd do it again——
JAKE: Once is enough, dearie!
ROXIE [*grinds her teeth in rage*]: "Through!" "Done
    with me!" I showed him, all right. If I don't have
    him, nobody does! [*Crumples, sobbing.*]
JAKE: I'm sure glad I met you tonight, sweetheart; to-
    morrow you'll sing another tune.
SERGEANT: Here's my confession—and the whole damn
    thing to do over again! [*Shakes* ROXIE.] Here, you,
    get your rags together! [*To* HARRISON.] We'll get
    her at the station, but let's finish him [*indicating*
    AMOS] now.
    [*He takes* AMOS *to adjoining room;* HARRISON
    starts to follow, but ROXIE *grasps his arm as he
    passes her.*]
ROXIE [*chattering*]: O God . . . God . . . Don't let
    'em hang me—don't. . . . Why, I'd . . . *die!*
    You promised—if I signed that . . . Can't—can't
    we—fix this up, you and me . . . fix it up . . .
    you know. . . .
HARRISON [*coldly, with virtuous glance toward* JAKE]:
    You don't frame anything with me!
    [*He shakes her off and goes into the next room.*]
JAKE [*looks down for a moment at* ROXIE, *who has*

burst into hysterical sobs, then speaks in pretended surprise]: Well, for cryin' out loud, did I ever! And what's the matter with *you!*

ROXIE: Matter? [*Half-shrieking.*] Matter? Are yuh crazy? [*Starts pacing up and down madly.*] O God, God, can't yuh *do* somethin'? Can't I get away, can't I——

JAKE [*takes her by shoulders and forces her back into chair*]: Keep your clothes on, kid.

ROXIE [*weeping*]: They will hang me, I know they will. I killed him and——

JAKE: What if yuh did? Ain't this Chicago? And gallant old Cook County never hung a woman yet! As a matter of fact—cold, hard statistics—it's 47 to 1 you'll go free.

ROXIE [*eagerly, as she starts packing her clothes in a suitcase*]: *Free?* How?

JAKE: Sure. Why, you're not even booked yet. But suppose they do, and the coroner's jury holds you, and you're sent to jail——

ROXIE [*shrieking*]: Jail! *Jail!* O God!

JAKE: Save them bedewzlin' tears for the jury, sister: for *jail's* the best beauty treatment in town. You take the rest cure for a couple uh months at the County's expense; you lay off men and booze till when you come to trial yuh look like Miss America. And that's when the big show starts! With you for leading lady! It's a hundred to one they clear you—that's straight goods. But suppose an off-chance *does* happen: your lawyer will appeal and Springfield, [*gnashing his teeth*] *dear* old Springfield! will reverse the decision like *that!* [*snaps his fingers.*] And if they don't, there's always a pardon—and you know our Governor!—God bless him! [*He tilts his chair back and smiles at her.*] There you are: a thousand to one—want to bet?

ROXIE [*fearfully*]: And you'll . . . *help* me?

JAKE: Sure! I'll phone Billy Flynn in the morning. He's the best criminal lawyer in town—next to Halliday. Specializes in women: freed Minnie Kahlstedt, the hammer murderess, Marcelle Wayne, who fed her children arsenic——

ROXIE: O yes, I read all about *them!*

JAKE: O he's a wonder, and will make it a real fight, for Harrison is an ace on the prosecutor's staff, and believe me, that boy won't leave a stone unturned to put you back of the bars! [*He smiles in satisfaction.*]

ROXIE: Well, you needn't be so *pleased*, if you really want me to go free.

JAKE [*stares at her*]: *Want* you to go free! How d'yuh get that way! Say, I'd give my last dollar—all three of 'em—and ever' night when I kneel down by my little bed I'll ask God to put a hemp rope around your nice white neck!

[*She shrinks back and he goes on in rapture.*] O baby, that would mean headlines six inches high— the story of the year! . . . But don't let my prayers worry you, kid, for God's not on the jury. . . . And with a face like yours—for Justice ain't so blind, in Chicago . . .

ROXIE [*pleased*]: O do you really think I'm—well—— [*Hesitates with coy modesty.*]

JAKE: Sure! I'm callin' you "the most beautiful murderess."

ROXIE: "Murderess!"

JAKE: Of course! What do you *think* I'd say? Prima donna?

ROXIE: But you needn't *say* it.

JAKE: Well, what the hell put you on front page? [*Impressively.*] Here you're gettin' somethin' money can't buy: front-page advertisin'. Why, a three-line want ad would cost you two eighty-five, and you'll get line after line, column after column, for nothin'. Who knows you now? Nobody. But this time tomorrow your face will be known from coast to coast. Who cares today whether you live or die? But tomorrow they'll be crazy to know your breakfast food and how did yuh rest last night. They'll fight to see you, come by the hundred just for a glimpse of your house—— Remember Wanda Stopa? Well, we had twenty thousand at her funeral.

ROXIE: I'm not interested in *funerals*.

JAKE [*grinning*]: Why, you may even end in wax works! Lord, girl, you're gettin' free publicity a movie queen would *die* for! Why, you'll be famous!

> [*The* SERGEANT *and* HARRISON *come to the door. The former motions to* ROXIE *and she goes with him to the adjoining room.* HARRISON *enters.*]

O baby, ain't we in luck though! A sweet story, a sweet story!

> [HARRISON *takes a flask from his pocket and pours two drinks. Solemnly they lift their glasses —the glasses of* ROXIE *and the dead man—in toast.*]

HARRISON: Here's to Roxie!

JAKE [*grinning*]: *Hang* her!

> [*They drink and he gives* HARRISON *an ecstatic shake.*]

Here I've just been prayin' for a nice, juicy murder —for two weeks now we haven't had nothin' but machine guns and hijackers.

[*They dump out dresser drawers, searching rap-idly for letters, pictures, etc.*]

And this one's got the makin's: wine, woman, jazz, a lover.

HARRISON [*tosses over diary*]: And plenty of dirt! Read 'em and blush.

JAKE [*flicks through it*]: O Roxie, Roxie . . . no mud on *her* shoes! . . . *He* must have been Number Four Sixty-eight!

HARRISON: And I can't bring it out in the trial.

JAKE: Ain't it hell. And me on a decent paper—God, what a waste! But gee, what a chance for you!

HARRISON: Just what I need; something big—sensational—to make me known.

JAKE: You've got it here. Scott will promote you on this.

HARRISON: Promote me—hell! It'll mean I can get out! For five years I've slaved like a dog for "justice and society" at three thousand a year. But now I've got my experience and this time next year I'll be rakin' in the shekels for "humanity and mercy"! That's where the money is: defense.

JAKE [*admiringly, taking notebook*]: Why, you old son-of-a-gun! . . . All right, let's have a quote from the rising young attorney.

HARRISON [*oratorically, kneeling before the debris from dresser*]: You may say: "It's a cold-blooded dastardly crime, for which Assistant State's Attorney Martin S. Harrison will ask the death penalty. . . ." A hanging case and I'm ready to go to the jury tomorrow!

JAKE: Atta boy! But Scott won't let you—not with election this fall! April . . . um . . . he'll hold it till September—say, if he could get a conviction, an

honest-to-God conviction, on a *woman*, why, he'd
sweep the city clean!

[*There's a ring at the door.* JAKE *answers while*
HARRISON *replaces dresser-drawers. It's the* PHO-
TOGRAPHER *with his flashlight outfit: another
rough and ready young man, with ingratiating
smile and steady flow of words.*]

BABE: Hello, Jake. What's it all about?

JAKE [*opens door for* SERGEANT *and* ROXIE]: Hot
stuff: she kills him rather than lose him.

BABE [*backs off and blinks his eyes in exaggerated appreciation of* ROXIE]: O my, my! Oi, oi! Ain't she
the prize-winner though! [*In pretended severity.*]
Keep them r. s. v. p. eyes off of *me*, sister; I'm a
married man. [*To* JAKE]. Where's the stiff?

JAKE: Outside—you don't want him.

SERGEANT: Hurry up, boys, we've got to get along.

BABE: Righto. This will make "the home" if we
hurry. [*Sets up his camera, takes flashlight powder,
etc.*] Any of the other boys been here? . . . Let's
see, what'll we have? One of you [*to* HARRISON]
and the girl—

SERGEANT: Say, she's *my* prisoner.

BABE [*fixes chairs*]: Both of you, and her in the center.

[HARRISON *and the* SERGEANT *both try for the
chair closest the camera.*]

JAKE: What about the husband?

BABE: Is there a husband? Sure, let's have the husband!

[HARRISON *steps to the door to call* AMOS, *and
the* SERGEANT *slips into the preferred chair.*]

Better give me the names, Jake.

[*He jots them in a notebook.* HARRISON *returns with* AMOS.]

AMOS: No, we don't. I'll bust his camera for him!

BABE: O you *will*, will you?

AMOS: This don't go in no papers!

BABE: O it *don't*, don't it!

AMOS: No, it don't. I won't let you use my name; this is to be kept quiet.

BABE: Say, shut up! ·[*To the others.*] Snap into it now: I gotta make a deadline.

AMOS: I won't have My Wife dragged into——

JAKE: Here, you, get this: We're not draggin' your wife—she dragged herself, see? You don't want publicity, but you're goin' to get it anyway. The question is: what kind? Do you want the papers for you or against you? Well, you gotta play ball!

BABE [*to* ROXIE]: You're willin', ain't yuh? [*She hesitates, and he looks astounded.*] Got Mary Pickford skinned a mile and don't want her pitcher in the paper! My God, can yuh beat it! You'll be right along with President Coolidge and Harold McCormick—there ain't a society dame in town but what would jump at the chance! [*He briskly guides her to the center chair.*] Right here now.

AMOS: Don't you do it, Roxie!

ROXIE: O shut up! I guess I will if I want to!

BABE [*at camera*]: That's the time—never let 'em boss you. And brush your hair back. It hides your eyes, and, believe me, you don't want to hide them eyes, does she, Jake?

ROXIE: I really need a marcel.

BABE: They're wearin' 'em straight. Now, Harrison, you and the Lieutenant look at her . . . *that's* right. And you [*to* ROXIE]—what's her name? Roxie?—look at the camera.

   [*He holds the powder high: the* SERGEANT

sprawls his hands and HARRISON *frowns judi-
ciously.*]

A little smile now, Roxie—just a little more. . . .
My, my, ain't that perfect, Jake? I'll bet she's the
girl on the toothpaste ad!

> [*Flash! Bang!* ROXIE *gives a little scream,*
> JAKE *opens the window to let out the smoke, and
> the men reluctantly give up their chairs.*]

All right, let's have another: her and the husband.

AMOS: Not *me!* I ain't goin' to have folks sayin'——

JAKE: Want 'em to think you're a yellah˙dawg and run
out on her? Come on here now and show the world
you're goin' to stand by her—it'll help her, won't it,
Babe?

BABE: Sure! When they see a man like *him*——

AMOS [*yielding*]: Well, uh course anything I can
do. . . .

BABE [*arranges them holding hands stiffly*]: *That's*
right. . . . You're askin' his forgiveness, and you
[*to* AMOS] smile down at her. . . . [*Back at the
camera.*] All right, let's go!

> [*Flash! Bang!* ROXIE *goes to the mirror and
> adds a bit more color all around.*]

Now I'd like one with the stiff——

SERGEANT: Say, Gazette, you've got enough!

BABE: One more, Captain, and I'm through! You're
here, makin' the arrest, and she's kneelin' by the
body. [*With a punch at* JAKE.] Down, Fido, play
dead!

JAKE [*flops on floor as suggested*]: Atta boy! I'll use
that for my lead!

ROXIE [*takes position as indicated*]: What do I do?

BABE: Cry—no, it's a shame to hide that face.

ROXIE: What about a profile?

BABE: Great!—But only half as good as a front; so yuh'd better look at the camera . . . *that's* right . . . and smile—just a little more—*big!* [*Flash! Bang!*] Done! [*Tosses things together and hurls goodbye.*] See yuh later, Jake!

SERGEANT [*takes* ROXIE *by the arm and turns to* JAKE]: Comin' with us?

JAKE: I'll drive over with Mart—gotta phone the office.
      [*The* SERGEANT *and* ROXIE, *followed by* AMOS, *go on out.*]

HARRISON [*stares after them*]: God, if I can only hang that woman!

JAKE: Well, you ain't got the chance of a snowball in hell! Dumb—but beautiful. [*He takes up phone.*] Dearborn O-five hundred. . . .

CURTAIN

ACT ONE

ACT I

*Sunday afternoon—two days later. Women's Ward of
the Cook County Jail, Chicago.*
*While the curtain is still down there is heard in heav-
ily accented tones the Salvation Army:*

> Be not dismayed what e'er betide,
> God will take *care* of *you;*
> Beneath His wond'rous *love* abide,
> God will take care of you.

*The curtain rises slowly on a large room, flanked on
each side [left and right] with tiny white bunk
rooms, equipped with cot, wash-stand, and chair. The
rear wall is a huge, double iron-screen, at which the
prisoners receive their friends and relatives on visiting days; in it [at the extreme left] is a double
locked door that opens into the hall around the elevator shaft. There's a small stand-table and a few
straight chairs at the right of this door, a long white
enamelled table with chairs on either side down the
center of the room. A stairway [invisible] at the
right [rear] leads up to the women's recreation and
lounging room.*
ROXIE *sits at the center table. She wears a jade green
satin dress, sleeveless; nude hose, decorated with
turquoise ribbon garters, and black velvet pumps. She
is pale—minus rouge, powder, and lipstick. There
is a box of cigarettes by her side and she smokes like
mad—straightforward, honest smoking, with appre-*

*ciative inhalation now and then. The table is stacked
with newspapers, and the floor strewn with discarded
sheets.*

MRS. MORTON [*the matron, in dark dress with large
white apron*] *sits across from her with scissors, ready
to clip any bit* ROXIE *designates. She's a stalwart
woman of fifty or so, with iron-gray hair, dark eyes
with flabby lids, ruddy complexion, and weak mouth.*

*Another woman lounges in a low rocker—a dark, quiet
woman in the late thirties, with smooth sallowed
features, large dreamy eyes, and full lips that have
a dipsomaniacal droop. She moves with studied lan-
guor and her voice is soft and low. She wears a heavy
dull crepe dress and topaz earrings that match
a certain tawny gleam in her smouldering eyes. She
is engrossed in the Society sheet while* ROXIE *pores
over the News sections.*

The voices of the singers [*several rooms away*] *ring
out fresh and clear, with a syncopation jazz can't
touch:*

> *God* will take *ca-are* of *you*
> Through *all* the *day*
> O'er *all* the *way*,
> He *will* take *ca-are* of *you*
> *God* will take *ca-are* of *you!*

ROXIE [*casually, as she hands* MRS. MORTON *another
paper to clip*]: Then yesterday must have been His
day off.

MATRON [*puzzled*]: What?

ROXIE: I just said God wasn't on the job at the inquest
or I wouldn't have landed here.
        [*The music starts up again.*]
Say, does that keep up all day?

MATRON: Just an hour or so. It's the Salvation Army—
the men likes to hear 'em. I'll have 'em close the
doors. [*Gets up and goes to the door.*]

ROXIE: With them squawkin', and the radio upstairs
tunin' in to Y.M. meetin's, health talks and ser-
mons. . . . [*As* MATRON *is out of earshot.*] This is
a helluva joint: Sunday here and not a drop uh liquor
in the house!

VELMA [*looks up in ready sympathy*]: That's the
hardest thing to get used to. [*Gives a little shiver
and takes another cigarette.*] Smoking helps
some.

ROXIE [*as* MATRON *returns*]: Look—*look!* [*Gives a
squeal of delight and points to page.*] A whole page
of pictures! [*Awed.*] Why, it's just like I was President or somethin': "Beautiful Roxie Hart, the Jazz-
Slayer"; "Roxie and Her Attorney"; "Roxie and
Her Husband"—[*Gives a gasp of surprise.*] For the
love uh—! *My Diary!* "The Little Book to Which
She Told Her Secrets"—can yuh beat it! . . .
"Only you and I, Diary, know how much we love
him. . . ." *Say,* who do you s'pose wrote that stuff?
You oughta see the *real* one!

VELMA [*darkly*]: They've got it all right. No sense of
—honor, reporters. Broke into my apartment the
night I—left, and stole a whole suit-case of letters—
valuable letters—letters from men who have loved
me. . . . [*She is overcome with emotion.*]

ROXIE: And a "Diagram of the Apartment"—my God!
See the spot marked X. [*Points with satisfaction.*]
That's where he fell—the dirty piker!

MATRON [*reprovingly.*]: Ssh, dearie! Mustn't talk
like that. [*To* VELMA.] She ain't seen her lawyer
yet.

ROXIE: Well, he *was*. [*Scornfully.*] One uh these wise guys that wants to be a Daddy on sixty a week and keep up a family on the side! But I called him all right!

MATRON: I know. . . . [*Virtuously.*] I never hear of a man's bein' killed but I know he got *just* what was comin' to him. . . . But you mustn't *say* it.

VELMA: What's your defense?

ROXIE [*shrilly*]: Defense? D'yuh think I'd let a guy hold out on me like that?

MATRON: But yuh can't tell the jury that!

ROXIE: O *can't* I!

VELMA: It's just like divorce: the *reason* don't count— it's the grounds.

ROXIE: Well, if that ain't grounds——

MATRON: But it's got to be accordin' to law, dearie: like he threatened or attackted you or somethin'.

ROXIE [*to* VELMA]: What's yours?

VELMA: Mine? Why, I didn't do it.

ROXIE: Then who did? There was jus' you and him in the room!

VELMA: I'm sure I don't know. I was drunk, my dear, dead drunk. Passed out completely and remember nothing from the time we left the café till the officers found me washing the blood from my hands. But I'm sure I didn't do it. . . . Why, I've the tenderest heart in the world, *haven't* I, Mrs. Morton?

MATRON: O she has indeed!

VELMA: And wouldn't hurt a worm. . . . [*Tremolo.*] Not even a *worm*. . . .

ROXIE: Is bein' drunk "grounds"?

MATRON: Now don't you worry, dearie, Billy Flynn will take care of all that.

ROXIE: He's comin' this afternoon.

MATRON [*wisely*]: He'll fix you up all right—they
don't make 'em any smarter than Billy. What he
don't know about juries and women——!
    [*A roll of her eyes intimates that the Britannica
    is a tyro.*]
He's the best in the city.
VELMA: Except Mr. Hessler.
MATRON [*hastily*]: Criminal lawyers, I mean.
ROXIE [*quickly, to* VELMA]: Ain't yours criminal?
VELMA: O dear, no—he's doing this *just* for me. Divorce
is his line. He's handled *all* of my cases—my family
attorney. [*Lifts brows languidly.*] *Very* exclusive.
ROXIE [*to* MATRON]: Is mine exclusive?
VELMA [*laughs scornfully*]: Billy?
MATRON [*hastily*]: Yes—in his way—yes. And he'll
give you a pretty trial.
ROXIE: Well, he ought to—for five thousand dollars.
MATRON: My, that's a lot of money—but it's worth
it. A cheap one could do it all right—why, with *your*
looks you don't need a lawyer at *all!* But it's a satisfaction to know it'll be done *right!* That's what I
said when I buried my husband.
ROXIE [*expectantly*]: Did you kill your——?
MATRON: Suicide it was. . . . I went in debt, but I
had all the trimmin's. . . . Never skimp on a funeral or a trial—especially a murder trial. Do it
right. [*Finishes clipping and counts the columns.*]
There! Five . . . eight . . . twelve . . . seventeen columns and twenty-three pictures—besides all
them they got this mornin'!
ROXIE [*takes one and reads with pleasure*]: "Roxie
Hart, the prettiest woman ever charged with murder
in Cook County, was held to the Grand Jury. . . ."
Ummm . . . [*runs on down column*] . . . "smiled

and cast coquettish glances from pansy eyes half hid by her purple turban"— [*Breaks off in anger.*] Can yuh beat it! I never wore a turban in my life! [*To* VELMA.] Why, I'd look as old as *you!*

VELMA [*affably*]: Yes; you gotta have chick for a turban.

[ROXIE *glares but has no answer.*]

MATRON: They're awful dumb, reporters. Never get anything right.

ROXIE [*continues reading*]: . . . "beige hose topped with turquoise garters"—say, they don't miss a trick!

MATRON: Garters! What next!

ROXIE: . . . "and rouged knees that warned Ann Pennington to look to her laurels."

VELMA: Well, it's the last rouge they'll see for some time.

ROXIE: Thank heavens, *I* can stand it, but it must be hard on people who're old or sallow. What's the big idea, anyway, shuttin' down on make-up?

MATRON [*apologetically*]: It's the rules, dearie, I don't know why. But you'll get it for the trial, all right. . . . O my, it's goin' to be a real pleasure to do *you!*

ROXIE [*takes up another clipping*]: "The wife of the dead man sat with bowed head during the inquest. . . ." Say, you oughta see her! And the clothes she wore! They'd oughta run our pictures together and call it "Why Men Leave Home." She must be all of forty, and fat. Men like 'em round but not fat. No pep, no life, while I'm always rarin' to go!

[*Continues reading.*] "But the jazz slayer showed neither grief nor remorse; powdered her nose and registered calm amusement——"

VELMA [*bitterly*]: You oughta cried and took on a lot. They razzed me the same way.

MATRON: Well, it's only the papers, and the jury's all *you* care about.

VELMA: And thank God they're *men!*

ROXIE [*flings down the clippings and springs up in rage*]: The nasty little cat on the *Ledger!* Calls me knock-kneed! I'll scratch her eyes out!

MATRON [*in alarm*]: O dearie, you mustn't get 'em down on you. Treat 'em nice and——

ROXIE: Well, they can't print lies about *me!*

VELMA: O can't they! If you think *you've* had a raw deal—tell her, Mrs. Morton.

MATRON: It's terrible, the things they wrote.

VELMA: Made fun of my jewels, yes, they did! Said my diamonds sparkled like real. *Like* real! An honest-to-God three-carat from my second husband —Mr. Phaley, you know him, the clothes manufacturer. And my emerald and platinum bracelet—a divorce present from my first. And my pearls—my real Japanese pearls . . .

MATRON: And your coat—don't forget your coat, Velma.

VELMA: A genuine Eastern mink, mind you, and they called it weasel! It was his—Mr. Clapp's—last gift to me before he—er—passed away.

ROXIE [*bewildered*]: Your husband?

VELMA: Such a generous man! Wonderful to me— more like a friend than a husband. That very night, just before he—went to his reward, he offered me two hundred a week alimony. I had just started my divorce, you know— O my dear, didn't you see that? All the papers had it, with pictures of me and everything. . . . And I said to him, "No, Clarence,

you're too generous—I won't take it." Quite firmly
I said it. "A hundred, yes, or maybe a hundred fifty;
and not over one seventy-five at the most." [*Triumphantly.*] Now in the face of that, is it likely I'd
—do what they said I did? Would I trade an offer
like that for a measly ten thousand insurance?—
Cigarette?

> [Roxie *holds up an empty box and* Velma *goes
> to the stairs.*]

Matron [*indignantly*]: Which the company won't pay.
Think of them holdin' out on her like that! O what
women suffers from men!

Roxie: But she *must* have killed him, for the papers
all said——

Matron [*severely*]: Now listen, dearie, if you're goin'
to believe what the papers say, you'll be suspicious of
ever'body here—includin' yourself. You'll get
along better if you just forget all that and take each
one as they come—that's my motto. . . . And as for
Velma, she's a pleasure to have around. No fightin',
no ugly language, refined and genteel—a real lady if
I ever saw one. And classy—all the papers say she's
the dressiest one we've ever had.

Roxie: She don't look like a sheba to me. She must be
forty, and dark and skinny. Men like 'em slim but
not skinny.

Matron [*with quick diplomacy*]: Well, of course she
ain't got *your* looks— O my, no! But she *is* a lady:
uses black narcissus perfume and never makes her
bed.

Roxie [*with a regretful glance at her bunk*]: I thought
you *had* to!

Matron: She hires Lucia——

Roxie: Who's Lucia?

[VELMA *returns with cigarettes.*]

MATRON: That Eyetalian woman——

ROXIE: —who chopped her husband's head off while the star boarder held him down?

VELMA: And she wasn't even drunk, my dear—not a drop!

MATRON [*reproachfully*]: Now, dearie, you mustn't be narrow-minded! [*In explanation to* ROXIE.] She's waitin' a new trial. They gave her fourteen years, but there's somethin' wrong with the indictment or other . . . Anyhow, here she is, and she does Velma's laundry——

ROXIE: I'll get her, too. And I won't make my bed, *either.* I'm just as good as——

MATRON [*hastily*]: Sure you are—both of you.

VELMA [*languidly*]: I've always had everything done for me. . . .

ROXIE [*recklessly*]: So have I! Ever'thing! A maid to bring in my breakfast——

VELMA: Really . . .

ROXIE: O yes, breakfast in bed *every* morning.

MATRON: Well, yuh gotta get up for your breakfast— that's rules—but yuh *can* have it brought in, from Wooster's just around the corner. Anything yuh want, only twenty dollars a week. And we'll all three eat together!

[*Song is heard again as the Army conducts its lively questionnaire:*

"Are your garments spotless?
Are they white as snow?
Are you washed in the blood of the Lamb?"

[*There appears at the end of the corridor, with scrubbing-brush and bucket, a small wiry woman*

*of forty or so, with a straggly mop of hair that
is the weird color left by many peroxides. Her
eyes are a washed-out blue, with now and then a
wild, fanatic gleam. Her mouth is broad, filled
with a fascinating mixture of natural and artificial
teeth. There are deep wrinkles—almost cuts—
around her mouth and eyes. She puts down her
bucket and stands surveying the women. Suddenly
she bursts into wild shrieks of mirthless, uncon-
tagious laughter. Shriek!—she bends double;
shriek!—she advances toward them.*]

LIZ [*gasp*]: O it's so funny! So funny!

MATRON: She's off again. Now, Liz——

LIZ [*gives* MATRON *a reassuring little pat*]: O no, I'm
not, don't you worry now. [*To others.*] But it's just
so *funny*. [*Starts again on a wild spasm of laughter.*]

MATRON: Hush! or I'll tell God on you.

LIZ [*subsides instantly*]: Aw, you wouldn't do that,
would you, Mrs. Morton? 'Cause it *is* funny.

ROXIE: What's funny?

LIZ: The three of us: you, her [*she points a skinny,
eczemaed hand toward* VELMA] and me all here together. They call you the prettiest, her the stylish-
est, and me the queer one—we all got our tags, so
folks will know us. We've come different roads:
mine's a long and hard one—it might have been different once—just once—but I went into a Far
Country. . . . [*Goes on in the sing-song call of the
revivalist.*] O God, O God, O God! . . . [*To
VELMA.*] Yours might have, too. Several times you
could have turned off, but dancing feet find sorrow.
[*To* ROXIE.] But you just took a short cut, that's all.

ROXIE: What are yuh talkin' about?

MATRON: She's off, don't mind her. Go on away, Liz.

Liz: She thinks I'm crazy. I am sometimes, but when I ain't [*her eyes flash triumphantly*] I got more sense 'an any of you. And right now, I *ain't*. I'm God's Messenger, that's what I am.

Matron: O my—she's awful when she starts on that.

Liz [*gaily*]: An' here we are now, the three of us! [*To* Velma.] You killed your husband for his insurance, [*to* Roxie] and you put a bullet in your lover when he got tired of you——

Roxie: That's a lie, you dirty——

Matron: Don't argue—it just makes her worse.

Liz: And I shot Jim . . . because he—[*her voice sinks to a hoarse whisper*]—laughed.

Velma: Because he wouldn't *marry* you.

Liz [*decidedly, alert again*]: Nope. I'd asked him lots of times—we'd been livin' in sin for seven years . . . years of the locust . . . but this time he *laughed*. [*Quietly.*] And I shot him. There was a candle sittin' on the floor—you know the Good Book says not to hide your light under a bushel—and he fell *right* by it. And I knelt beside him and prayed. . . .

Matron: Look out for them that's allus readin' the Bible and prayin'. Somethin's wrong *some* place.

Liz [*back in the revivalist character again*]: And here we are, stained with the blood that only the Lamb of God can cleanse: murderesses . . . murderesses!

Velma: Shut up, you fool! You're not—*that*, unless you're *convicted*.

Liz: O yes, you are! It don't take no trial. I was a murderess the minute Jim fell. God judged me then, right then. I can see Him now . . . [*her eyes grow glassy, and her voice is shrill in horror*] sittin' there on His throne . . . [*Gives a wild shriek.*]

MATRON [*rises and takes her by the arm*]: Come on, now, that's enough out of you. Upstairs now—go 'long! [*Takes her shrieking to the stairs.*]

ROXIE: Well, that's a cheerful little playmate. What's *her* defense?

VELMA: Insanity.

ROXIE: Is bein' *crazy* "grounds"?

VELMA [*nods*]: But it may mean the asylum . . . and besides, it's so embarrassing——

MATRON [*returns with pack of cards from table*]: Thank God, there ain't many like her! . . . Well, girls, what about a hand? [*To* ROXIE.] Are you good at bridge?

ROXIE: Better at poker.

MATRON: O no, dearie, bridge is all we play—penny a point.

[*The bell rings, and she goes to answer.*]

VELMA: She always wins.

ROXIE: From you, maybe; but watch little Roxie, the girl gambler.

VELMA: All right; but I warned you.

ROXIE: *Warned* me? . . . Oh! You mean I've got to *let* her win?

VELMA: Suit yourself.

ROXIE: Well, I'll be damned.

MATRON [*calls from door*]: It's your husband, Mrs. Hart.

ROXIE [*springs up*]: Did he bring my clothes? [*Reaches for the battered suit-case the* MATRON *holds.*]

MATRON: I have to look at 'em first, to be sure there's nothin' concealed. [*Returns to table, followed by* ROXIE.] Ain't yuh goin' to talk to him? [ROXIE *looks blank.*] There at the screen.

VELMA [*bitterly, to* ROXIE]: That's your reception room: you play peek-a-boo through the bars.

ROXIE [*to* MATRON, *who's inspecting the clothes*]: Leave out the purple bengaline if—[*goes to screen.*] Amos, did you bring the purple bengaline?

> [*Evidently he answers, but the words are undistinguishable.*]

My God! Can't you do nothin' right? . . . Terrible! . . . Locked up all night in one of them sardine boxes. . . . And I have to wash in cold water! . . . What the hell are *you* walkin' the floor about? You got it easy, while I'm locked up here with God's Messenger!

> [*There's a flash and explosion outside: the* CAMERAMEN *have their picture of* AMOS *at the screen.*]

MATRON [*hurries to the door*]: It's them blame photographers!

> [ROXIE *and* VELMA *preen for pictures.*]

Now, boys, none uh that!

BABE [*outside*]: Hello, Mrs. Morton! I got my ticket, all right!

MATRON [*nods toward* AMOS]: But not him. It's against the rules—you know that, Mr. Maloney: relatives is never allowed inside.

BABE: But just for a little pitcher? Have a heart, Mrs. Morton! Just this once—the first day, you know—with you here beside 'em——

> [MATRON *opens the door, and* BABE *enters, followed by* AMOS.]

Come on, Obadiah! What—Amos? All right, Amos.

> [VELMA *goes upstairs at a nod from* MATRON; BABE *blows* ROXIE *a kiss and starts to set up*

camera; Amos *makes a dash for* Roxie, *who starts to match his ardor but sees the camera is not quite ready.*]

Amos: Roxie! My wife!

Babe: Wait a minute, wait a minute!

Amos: How do they treat you? By God, just remember this: [*strides up and down, glaring fiercely*] I ain't gonna have my wife——

Matron [*dangles keys*]: Looky here, young man, out you *go!*

Babe: Don't mind him—they dropped him when he's a baby. [*To* Amos.] Keep your clothes on, Habba-kuk. She's sittin' pretty and havin' the time of her young life, all for nothin'.

Roxie: For nothin'! Say, boy, you've been readin' the wrong ticker!

Babe: Now: hold 'em again, Hart! As you were!

[Amos *and* Roxie *resume stiff embrace.*]

That's right. Face the camera, and smile, just a little smile . . .

[*Flash! Bang!*]

Now you here at the table. [*Clears it of papers.*] Ain't you the lucky girl, though, with all these pitchers! And you can thank your stars you're in Chi-cago where the poor workin' girl's got a chance. In New York now, yuh gotta be a millionaire to make front page. You could shoot up the whole town and nobody gives a damn unless you're in the Social Register!

[Roxie *flounces down on top of the table, cross-ing her feet.*]

That's right: we want them million-dollar knees! More——

[*She lifts skirt.*]

Just a little more!

[*Flash! Bang!*]

Done! [*Gathers up equipment.*] And I won't see you no more, sister, till the Judgment Day! S'long!

[Matron *lets him out.*]

Roxie [*at table with* Amos]: All right then, I'll eat with the wops and niggers!

Amos [*thundering*]: No, you don't! My wife'll have the best there is! Twenty a week—hell, what's that! I got a raise—fifty-five now.

Roxie: My God!

Amos: Sure, the boss has been swell to me: offered me a week's vacation, and when I got back from the inquest the whole office crowded around, and shook hands with me, and wished me luck.

Roxie: Well, it's just because you're my husband. You'd be nobody if it wasn't for me!

Amos [*indignantly*]: It's because I'm sticking *by* you. I guess there's not many guys would do it.

Roxie: Well, whatever it is, you got a raise out of it, didn't you? And I've *got* to have money, for laundry and makin' beds, and cigarettes,—and you know how a penny a point counts up!

Amos: Say, looky here!

Roxie [*shrilly*]: Do you want me to look like a cheap skate before all these people? All right, all right. There's plenty of money in the world, you know, and you ain't got no corner on it. God, why did I ever marry you!

Amos [*takes out wallet and begins counting bills*]: Will ten do?

Roxie: Yes—twenty! [*Gives a generous grab for the money.*]

Amos [*in alarm*]: Yeah, but what about *me?*

Roxie: My God, can't yuh think uh nothin' but yourself?

[*The bell rings and there is heard outside a rich voice, hypnotic in its suggestive power, with a minor undertone that's Gaelic:* "Well, well, Mrs. Morton!"]

[*He enters—our hero, counsel for the defense,* BILLY FLYNN. *He's a little man, like Napoleon, and he carries himself with the Corporal's air. A magnificent iron-gray mane, with a forelock he tugs at to convey the impression of thought, or tosses back now and then to reveal the Cæsarian brow. The eyes are deep-set and keen; the nose starts out to be Semitic, but ends with an Irish tilt; the mouth is broad without being generous, and the jaw is pugilistic.*

[*He is dressed with careful carelessness: tweed topcoat and fedora, pepper and salt sack-suit, blue shirt with soft collar, and striped necktie with golden horseshoe. He buys on Michigan Boulevard, but follows the style of West Chicago. A millionaire would know his tailor, but a bricklayer would feel comfortably that his Sunday clothes beat Billy's.*]

Matron [*in note of tragedy*]: Oh, Mr. Flynn, the photographer's just gone!

Flynn: That's all right: he got me downstairs.

Matron: The husband's here, too.

Flynn: Good! *Just* the man I want to see!

[*She goes down the corridor at the left, and he stalks by* Roxie *without a word or look, straight to her husband.*]

Well, Hart? [Amos *turns.*] And what about me?

Amos [*grandly*]: Have a chair.

FLYNN [*ignores invitation and repeats*]: What about me?

AMOS: I—I didn't do quite as well as I hoped.

FLYNN: No?

AMOS: But I will, all right, I will. [*Takes certificates, books, etc., from pocket.*] Here's five hundred on my insurance.

ROXIE [*shrilly*]: Cashin' your insurance? Not much you don't! That's mine!

[FLYNN's *hand reaches it first.*]

FLYNN: That makes a thousand.

AMOS: Yes, sir. And three hundred that I borrowed— [*gives it to* FLYNN] and seven hundred out of the building and loan——

FLYNN: Two thousand.

AMOS: And—and that's all I've got—*so far.*

FLYNN [*watching him keenly*]: What about her father?

AMOS: I phoned him yesterday—long distance—and— he'll probably raise some later.

FLYNN [*bites his cigar and snaps out his words with an "ugly" look*]: You damned liar! I phoned him, too, last night . . . And he told me just what he told *you:* that she went to hell six years ago and she could stay there forever before he'd spend one cent to get her out!

ROXIE [*to* AMOS]: I told yuh not to try him.

FLYNN: Now I don't give a damn where you get the money—that's your problem. Beg it, borrow it— any way. . . .

AMOS: I'll pay you twenty a week——

ROXIE: And where do *I* come in, you big stiff? What about *me?*

FLYNN: Shut up, you ——!

[ROXIE *subsides.*]

AMOS: I'll give you notes with interest—double—till ever' cent——

FLYNN: No, you don't. None uh that installment stuff. I wouldn't be *bothered* with your chicken-feed. I play square, Hart, dead square. When you came to me yesterday I didn't say, "Is she innocent, is she guilty, will it be an easy case or a hard one?" *Nothing* like that, now *did* I! No. I said: "Have you got five thousand dollars?" And you said, "Yes." [*Eyes him in contempt.*] You dirty liar! . . . And I took your case—and I'll *keep* it. But she'll rot in jail before I bring it to trial!

ROXIE [*angrily, to* AMOS]: See what you've done, you big——

AMOS [*trying to be nonchalant*]: You needn't worry about your money—you'll get it all right.

FLYNN [*in well-simulated rage*]: Get out! Get *out!* And don't come near me again till you've got three thousand in your fist!

AMOS: Well—so long, Roxie. [*Starts to kiss her but she pushes him away.*]

ROXIE: Can the soft stuff.

AMOS: See you Thursday.

ROXIE: And don't forget my dinner *now*—from Woosters' p.d.q.!

[AMOS *goes slowly, and she softens her tone as she turns to the lawyer.*]

Listen: you didn't mean what you said about delayin' my case, did yuh?

[FLYNN *takes a cigar and doesn't answer.*]

Couldn't—*I*—pay you?

FLYNN [*unconcerned*]: That depends on your bank account.

ROXIE [*softly, laying her hand on his arm*]: I mean—couldn't we be—*friends?*

FLYNN [*vigorously*]: Good! You've got that out of your system. Now listen: I'm not interested in your looks, your age, your sex—nothing *except* as it affects the case. You mean just one thing to me: five thousand dollars. Get that.

ROXIE [*takes the slap philosophically, lights a cigarette, reseats herself on the table*]: Suit yourself. But if you change your mind . . .

FLYNN: Forget it. [*Draws up chair and goes on in business-like tone.*] Now: that sob sister from the *Evening Star* is coming.

ROXIE: Mary Sunshine?

FLYNN: And the woman from the *Ledger*.

ROXIE: I won't see her.

FLYNN: You've talked so much, you can't stop now. [*Grimly.*] If you tell enough lies they're bound to forget a few!

ROXIE: But not *her*—I'll be damned if I do!

FLYNN [*pleasantly*]: You'll be hanged if you don't. . . . And by the way, pipe down on that swearing. What we've got to do now is go out for sympathy through the press. The story of your life starts tomorrow in the *Star:* "From Convent to Jail."

ROXIE: *What?*

FLYNN: My secretary's writing it this afternoon—signed with your name, of course.

ROXIE: Gee, an authoress!

FLYNN: Beautiful Southern home, every luxury and refinement, [*she listens with interest*] parents dead, educated at the Sacred Heart, fortune swept away, runaway marriage . . . [*Severely.*] You're a lovely, innocent child bewildered by what has happened. Young, full of life, lonely, you were caught up by the mad whirl of a great city—she gives a red-hot picture of cabaret life—that jazz stuff is always good. . . . And you were drawn inevitably like a moth to the flame! [ROXIE *drinks it in open-mouthed.*] And now the mad whirl has ceased: a butterfly crushed on the wheel. . . . And you sob with remorse for the life you have taken——

ROXIE: O God!

FLYNN: Cut out "God"—stay where you're better acquainted. . . . And don't overdo it. Go as far as you like with Mary Sunshine—she'll swallow hook, line, and sinker, for it's what *she* wants, but easy with the *Ledger* woman. The important thing is *regret.* You're *sorry—sorry:* you'd give your life gladly to bring him back.

ROXIE [*drops pose*]: Say, why did I do it? What's my defense? Was I drunk or crazy?

FLYNN [*shakes head*]: Nobody cares about a lunatic unless they've got money. Whenever they ask "why," all you remember is a fearful quarrel, he threatened to kill you. You can see him coming toward you with that awful look in his eyes—that *wild* look! And—get this now: you *both* grabbed for the gun. See? Self-defense. Whatever else we weave in afterwards, *that's* there from the start. . . . You've spent a sleepless night—tossing about——

ROXIE: Walking the floor——

[*The bell rings and* FLYNN *looks down the corridor.*]

FLYNN: Here's Sunshine now. [*With look of dismay at* ROXIE's *brilliant garb.*] O my God, that dress!

ROXIE [*resentfully*]: What's the matter with it?

FLYNN: You ought to have something simple—plain—
dark.
ROXIE: Wait a minute! [*Dashes to suit-case and waves
a black dress at him.*] How's this?
FLYNN [*nods*]: And slick down your hair. [*As she starts
off.*] And don't forget: regret, remorse——
ROXIE: I got you! "And we both grabbed for the gun!"
[*She runs lightly upstairs with the dress clasped
in her arms, as the* MATRON *admits* MARY SUN-
SHINE, *who is really Pollyanna's older sister. She
is a soulful semi-blonde with protruding front
teeth and adenoids, who talks with a slightly af-
fected lisp and boundless enthusiasm.*]
FLYNN [*holds out a hand but doesn't rise*]: Well, here
she is: Sunshine herself. Nice little story you had
last night.
SUNSHINE: Isn't this *wonderful!* You're *just* the person
I want to see! How *is* she today?
FLYNN [*shakes his head gravely*]: Terrible strain, terrible; but she's a brave little woman.
SUNSHINE: O I feel so *sorry* for her when I think of all
she must have gone through to be driven to a step
like that.
FLYNN: Only a woman can understand.
SUNSHINE: But she has everyone's sympathy—that will
help her in this awful hour. [*Fumbles in bag and
brings out a handful of telegrams and letters.*]
We're paying ten dollars a day for the best letter,
you know, and some of these are just too lovely. I
cried and cried over this one. [*Hands him letter on
pink paper with purple ink.*]
FLYNN [*reads gravely, quoting line now and then*]:
. . . "the old heart-breaking story . . ." . . .
"there but for the grace of God go I . . ." . . .

"and the woman always pays." . . . True. True.

SUNSHINE: And here's one that's just darling: from five college boys, and they clubbed together and sent her a huge box of roses and lilies. Isn't that sweet? It's too bad they won't let her have flowers—there are eight boxes downstairs now!

MATRON [*comes in from corridor followed by* JAKE]: Just run on up, Miss Sunshine.

SUNSHINE: O *may* I?·[*Goes on upstairs.*]

JAKE [*waves friendly salute to* FLYNN, *and smiles cynically after* SUNSHINE]: Little Sunshine gathering tears!

FLYNN: Nice little story this morning, Jake.

JAKE [*pulls up chair*]: Used your name six times!

FLYNN [*takes flask and pours drink*]: Yeah—nice little story.

JAKE [*drinks*].: Anything new?

FLYNN [*shakes head*]: Indictment tomorrow, of course. [*Drinks.*]

JAKE: Bail?

FLYNN: *Bail?* Hell, no! They ain't even got money for *me!* A fine case you got me!

JAKE [*grins*]: Well, charge it up to publicity—you'll get enough.

FLYNN: O no, Henry. I like to see my name in print all right, but it don't take the place of the little old dollar: *cash* in *advance*. And so far this guy hasn't scraped up but two thousand.

JAKE: *Say!* Why not a sale?

FLYNN: Sale?

JAKE: Sure—an auction. They got four rooms of junk.

FLYNN: Second-hand furniture don't bring enough to——

JAKE: But look whose it is! You should have seen 'em

at Maldoon's! Furniture, books, clothes, everything
at triple prices. And *he* was nothin' but a get-rich-
quick fake—another Ponzi, while this girl is Chicago's latest slayer—or was the last time I phoned
the office.

FLYNN [*thoughtfully*]: That's not a bad idea.

JAKE [*indignantly*]: It's the best little idea on La Salle
Street! *IF* her stuff's paid for. Call her down.

FLYNN [*bellows at foot of stair*]: Mrs. Hart! Roxie!

JAKE: Why, they'll go *wild* at the chance to own a tea-
cup drank out of by a real live murderess—and of
course if she dies by due process of law, the value is
enhanced! We could use a carload of underwear!
And victrola records—I'll kill a chicken over 'em—
think of owning the record she played while the Boy
Friend lay dying! [*Slaps* FLYNN *on the back.*]
Great stuff, Billy, great stuff!

FLYNN: Go to it, kid, if you can raise my three thousand.

> [ROXIE *enters. She wears a black dress, yes, but
> sleeveless with huge scarlet flower on one shoulder
> and hula-hula skirt of red fringe. Her hair, glis-
> tening from a wet brush, lies smooth like a medi-
> eval saint's, and she turns sad eyes from* FLYNN *to*
> JAKE.]

JAKE [*excitedly*]: Say, is it paid for—your furniture?

ROXIE [*drops the sad pose and flops into a chair*]: My
God, are they comin' *here!* Tell 'em they got the
wrong party, that I'm out, that—that— [*Gives up.*]
Can you beat it! No respect for grief at all.

JAKE: O hell!

ROXIE: I used to hang crepe on the door, but it never
worked more'n once.

JAKE [*rallies, to* FLYNN]: O well—what's a few

hundred! [*To* ROXIE.] Listen, kid: we're goin' to
have an auction and sell off your things.

ROXIE [*sits up*]: Like *hell* you are!

FLYNN [*coolly*]: Like hell we *are!*

ROXIE: Well, there's not enough to pay you, even if—
[*Hastily.*] My things are grand, *perfectly grand,* but
you'd never get what I paid for 'em.

JAKE [*solemnly*]: Five times as much!

[*She stares; he takes auctioneer's stand and
holds up imaginary articles.*]

The mirror of Marie Antoinette . . . Carrie Na-
tion's hatchet . . . the bed of Roxie Hart . . .
why, they're museum pieces, my dear!

ROXIE [*squirms with delight*]: Museum pieces, O gee!

JAKE: Sure: you're famous! Why, the rubberneck
busses are already cryin': "Half a block to your left
is the home of Roxie Hart, the beautiful jazz-
slayer!"

ROXIE [*genuinely impressed*]: My God . . . tell my
husband that, won't you? He thinks it's *him.*

JAKE: And they're tearin' up the shrubbery for sou-
venirs.

ROXIE [*with animation*]: There's a lot uh poker chips
and cards that'd be cute for that. And little ash-trays
—that we used that night . . .

JAKE [*nodding*]: His last ashes.

ROXIE [*gives a little cry*]: Oh! And all my dresser
things!

JAKE: O Lord, yes! There's a fortune there!

ROXIE: The crystal bottles and atomizer——

JAKE [*holds aloft*]: "The mystic perfume that lured
young Casely from his home—what am I offered?
Twenty—thirty—the magic scent"——

ROXIE: I always use black narcissus. . . . And my

jewels: An honest-to-God three carat, and a dia-
mond and platinum bracelet and pearls—real Japanese pearls——

FLYNN [*alert, to* JAKE]: We'd better keep them out.

JAKE [*nods*]: And passing on to the wearing ap-
parel. . . .

ROXIE [*firmly*]: Wait. If I sell my clothes——

FLYNN: And you're going to.

ROXIE: The first five hundred dollars goes to buy more.

FLYNN: *After* my fee.

JAKE: *After* the furniture people.

ROXIE: After *nothin'*. It's *my* clothes and it's 'cause I
wore 'em that they're museum pieces. The *first* five
hundred. My God, do you think I'm a Kewpie?

FLYNN: You *will* need a different get-up for the trial.

ROXIE: There's a winter coat with caracul fur——

JAKE: To hell with your winter coat: how much underwear have you got?

ROXIE [*beams*]: Oh, there's a closet *full* of them! Rose
with fur all around it, and a green georgette, and the
blue—you know: the one I wore the night [*with
triumphant look at* FLYNN] "we both grabbed for
the gun!"

JAKE [*regretfully*]: Unfortunately the blue is State's
Exhibit B.

ROXIE: And dozens and dozens of— [*Scurries to the
suit-case.*] Here, take these, too! [*Lays a few garments aside, then tosses rest back in case.*] Take 'em
all and bring me some new ones *quick!* [*Pauses, gives
herself a reflective wriggle, then stoops and swiftly
removes her garters.*]

JAKE [*waves them aloft*]: Bravo! "You've read about
'em, boys, here they are: what am I offered for the
Famous Turquoise Garters?" [*Breaks off in alarm as*

she seems bent on further disapparelment.] Stop!
This is *not* strip poker!

ROXIE [*straightens with dignity*]: I was only *rollin'* my
stockin's. [*They drop to her ankles and* JAKE *re-
treats.*]

FLYNN [*with look toward stair*]: Sunshine's coming!

JAKE [*hastily grabs suit-case*]: Remember, kid: this is
my story!

ROXIE [*nods*]: The first five hundred!

    [*She sits at table rolling hose as they leave and*
SUNSHINE *comes down the stairs.*]

SUNSHINE [*flutters in, pauses a moment at sight of the
curiously bent figure—rolling hose—then goes to
her*]: My dear, O my dear, what *is* it?

ROXIE [*lifts sweet tragic face*]: I've given all—all
that a woman can give . . .

SUNSHINE [*grabs notebook*]: Yes—yes: you've given
your all . . .

ROXIE: And now the mad whirl is over—a butterfly
crushed on the wheel—*you* know: a butterfly . . .
moth and the flame . . . [*with that lovely wistful
smile.*]

SUNSHINE [*scribbles*]: And what caused you to——

ROXIE [*sadly, with* LIZ' *mystic intonation*]: It might
have been different once . . . but dancing feet find
sorrow . . .

SUNSHINE: "Dancing." Er—jazz? The Charleston?
Shall we say the Charleston, Mrs. Hart? And er—
drink—you *had* been drinking?

ROXIE [*with* VELMA's *ease*]: O yes, I was drunk, my
dear, dead drunk!

SUNSHINE: O lovely, lovely—my paper's dry, you
know! . . . So you would advise girls to avoid jazz
and drink. What else, Mrs. Hart? How did you hap-

pen to . . . just *why* did you . . . shoot . . .

ROXIE [*grows dramatic*]: I was mad—crazy—insane!

SUNSHINE: O dear!

ROXIE [*hastily*]: Not enough for the asylum, you know
—over with right away.

SUNSHINE [*nods*]: Temporary insanity.

ROXIE: For I really have the tenderest heart in the
world—wouldn't hurt a worm . . . not even [*with*
VELMA'S *tremolo*] a worm. . . .

SUNSHINE [*sympathetically*]: And what brought it on?

ROXIE [*her eyes grow dark and her emotion rises*]: He
—he threatened my life. . . .

SUNSHINE: What a terrible man!

ROXIE: O he *was! Very terrible!*

MATRON [*enters with two monstrous baskets, one tied
with pink ribbon, which she places on the table and
examines*]: It's your supper—two of 'em.

ROXIE [*looks blank*]: Two?

MATRON: One from Woosters' and a fancy chicken dinner from *some*place, with a note.

ROXIE [*opens and reads*]:

"My heart and hand are at your feet,
With you my life would be complete.
                    Yours, with pleasure—
                    An Unknown Admirer."

Poetry! Ain't that romantic!

SUNSHINE [*takes note*]: I'll thank him for you through
the paper.

ROXIE [*arranges food*]: You might tell him, too, that
I like *Russian* dressing. . . . Shortcake—say, he's
a regular guy!

[MATRON *disappears with other basket.* ROXIE

falls to eating heartily, and SUNSHINE *watches fascinated.*]

SUNSHINE: They'll all be so *glad* to know you can *eat.*

ROXIE [*stops short and resumes "character"*]: It's choking me, every mouthful . . . but I feel it's my duty. . . .

SUNSHINE: O it *is!* You *must* keep your strength!

ROXIE [*forces herself to a more languid pace*]: The first bite I've tasted since . . . he went to his reward . . . [*Presses handkerchief to her eyes.*]

SUNSHINE [*pats her hand*]: *Dear* Mrs. Hart!

ROXIE: O, if I could only bring him back! How gladly . . . how gladly I'd give my own life! [*Chokes with emotion, takes a few healthy bites.*] And sleep—I can't sleep either. . . . *All* night I walked about —tossing the floor. . . .

SUNSHINE: O my *dear.*

ROXIE [*in hollow tone*]: Always his face coming toward me . . . [*her emotion rises as she lives through it all*] with that terrible look—that *wild* look—in his eyes . . . We both grabbed for the gun! [*She reaches forth her hand and clasps a roll of bread.*]—And I shot [*dramatic pause*]—to save my honor!

[*The Salvation Army starts up again:*]

"In the sweet bye-and-bye,
We shall meet on that beautiful shore;
In the sweet bye-and-bye. . . ."

Ain't it grand—the Salvation Army! I love to hear 'em: I'm awful refined. . . . You see, I was born in a convent. . . . [*Continues talking and eating, while* SUNSHINE *writes, as*

THE CURTAIN FALLS

ACT TWO

ACT II

Same scene, one month later—early afternoon of May the third.

A stolid figure in blue calico sits sewing by the great end windows; LIZ, *with bucket and brush, is busy scouring the floor; through the half-opened bunk-door can be seen a reclining figure that looks very much like our friend* ROXIE. *The center of the stage, however, both physically and emotionally, is held by* VELMA, *who stands on top of one of the white tables and turns slowly while the* MATRON *turns up the hem of her dress, making it now a good twenty inches instead of sixteen from the floor.*

It is a new VELMA—*ten years at least have gone from her age. Smooth, lithe, clear-eyed, and well-groomed. Her shingle bob fairly glistens with something or other, and there is a touch of tangerine rouge (from the huge make-up box on the table) on each soft cheek, and her lips are arched in a scarlet bow that matches her dress of lipstick red, which certainly catches the eye. At present she is in the agony of suppressed hysterics. Tears would spoil her make-up and uncontrolled rage distort her face, so she keeps a calm mask and rolls out a continuous flow of bitter invective in a gentle monotone.*

VELMA: Damn Marshall Field!

MATRON [*punches dress so* VELMA *can feel where it stops*]: Is that short enough?

Liz [*pauses for a glance and giggles*]: O my, *that'll* bring the jury to your feet all right!

Roxie [*comes out from her bunk and leans against door-sill, eying* Velma *with venom*]: My God, what house have they *raided* now! [Velma *wheels and* Liz *giggles*.] So loud it woke me up. Lord, I'll bet ever' bull in the stockyards hears it and is gnashin' his teeth!

Velma [*tearfully, to* Matron]: It's true. . . . Think of it; their last picture of me in *this! Damn* Marshall Field [*points trembling to empty suit-box on table*] —to send an empty box!

Matron [*peers in box again while* Roxie *looks like the kitty that's gulped a canary*]: Queerest thing I ever heard of—just a bunch of tissue paper, not even the bill. But you can get your money back——

Velma: *Money!* What the *hell* do I care for *money!* It goes to the jury this afternoon and—I can't *stand* it!

Matron: Now, dearie—it's certainly got *style.*
　　　[Roxie *snorts.*]

Velma: But what's *that?* The other had *meaning.* Mr. Hessler picked it himself: a beautiful soft green that would stand out in the crowded courtroom—you never *saw* such a crowd!

Liz: I had a crowd, too.

Velma: But not like mine.

Liz [*shrilly*]: I did, too—didn't I, Mrs. Morton!

Velma [*ignoring her*]: Every seat taken, the hallway jammed——

Roxie: A lot *you* know about crowds! Now at my auction——

Liz [*screams*]: Shut up about your old auction!

Roxie: There were thousands and *thousands*——
Liz: How do *you* know?
Roxie: The papers all *said* so, didn't they, Mrs. Morton?
Liz: Yeah—and they're a bunch uh durned liars. [*Complacently, to* Velma.] We *see* our crowds, don't we.
Roxie: A handful in a courtroom!
Matron: There's hundreds of 'em——
Velma: *Thousands!*
Liz: MILLIONS!
Roxie [*in impotent rage*]: You God-damned bunch of four-flushers!
Matron [*bangs her hand down on table*]: Now, Roxie.
Roxie [*goes in cell*]: Aw, tie it outside!
Matron: If you've got a headache, sleep it off; if you ain't, go on upstairs where you belong. I've had enough raggin' out uh you today.
Roxie [*turns for a last shot*]: Anyway they *paid* for my auction and that's the rancid test. While *you're* just a free show—that's all! [*Bangs the door.*]
Liz [*chants in sing-song*]: "Roxie's mad and I'm glad . . ."
Matron: Shut up.
Liz [*returns to scrubbing*]: Jealous, that's what she is—jealous.
Roxie [*re-opens the door, with dignity*]: When My Lawyer comes——
Matron [*looks up from hemming process*]: Now get that out of your head. Mr. Flynn ain't got time to be runnin' over here whenever you take a notion——
Roxie [*loftily*]: This ain't a notion—it's something *very* important.

LIZ: Wants in the papers, that's what it is.

ROXIE: And he *is* coming; I sent word by Mary Sunshine. [*Slams the door after her.*]

VELMA: The next time she butts in on an interview the way she did this morning—my *God*, can't you hurry!

LIZ: Maggie an' me never dolled up this way, *did* we, Maggie?

[*The figure in the rocking-chair doesn't answer.*]

MATRON: Yeah, an' look what yuh *got*, too: the rest of your life in Joliet.

LIZ [*shrilly*]: I don't care, I told 'em what I thought, didn't I—the Judge an' jury, ever'body. [*Flings her arms out in dramatization.*] "Hang me," I said, that's what I said, "Build a platform right down at State and Madison and invite the whole town—reserved seats for ever'body, so they can all come, and have a good time." That's what I said, right to the Judge! [*To* VELMA.] And that's more'n *you've* done, for *all* your clothes! You ain't said a word now, have you, not a word!

VELMA: My lawyer won't let me.

LIZ: Yeah—he knows once you opened your mouth they'd hang you.

VELMA: That's a lie! They can tell just by *looking* at me I'm a lady. That's why it's so important what I wear . . . something quiet and refined . . . the green would have been just right. . . . [*Suddenly.*] This won't do—it simply won't *do!* [*Ready to cry, she jumps down from the table.*] Oh, I could *kill* Marshall Field! [*Stalks upstairs in rage.*]

[*The bell rings,* MATRON *answers and* ROXIE *peeps out from cell.*]

ROXIE: Is that Mr. Flynn?

LIZ: Say, what're you gonna do: make a will?

Roxie [*darkly*]: It's all *right* what I'm goin' to do—I *want* him.

Liz: Humph . . . "Roxie's mad and I am glad . . ."

Matron [*calls from door*]: Maggie—you. At the screen.

> [*Figure at window starts up bewildered. She's a rough peasant type, thirty-five or so, with straggly black hair and large plain features.*]

Liz [*nods toward screen*]: Go on—it's your husband and kid.

> [Maggie *gives a guttural cry, drops her sewing in the chair, and scurries heavily to the screen.* Liz *trails after her. The* Matron *is still at the door and no one is looking:* Roxie *comes out from her cell with the green dress she has stolen, runs quickly and puts it back in the Marshall Field box; then extracts lipstick from make-up box and hurls it through the bars as* Jake *and the* Matron *enter. She then melts away to her cell.*]

Matron: Velma's dressing—do you want to see her?

Jake [*throws admission card on table*]: No, thanks, I'm waiting for this one.

Matron [*reads card*]: My land, are they sendin' *her?*

Jake [*grins*]: Due this afternoon from the Desplaines station. And she's a hell-cat for sure! That's what they call her: "Go-to-hell Kitty!"

Matron [*tragically*]: On top of ever'thing else!

Jake [*tosses hat on table and takes chair*]: *What* else?

Matron: Two convictions this week—ain't it *turrible?* That allus gives ever'body the blues.

Jake: Well, Velma will cheer 'em up: *she's* gettin' away with murder all right. Why, the Judge himself says she's the classiest one he's ever had!

Matron: Well, I hope so! Another day of this dressin'

and I'll be goin' crazy! . . . [*Goes on down the corridor.*] What a life, what a life!

Liz [*unconsciously imitating the matron*]: An' on top uh all that Roxie sulkin' like the devil!

Jake: Roxie?

Liz [*lowers voice with warning look toward* Roxie's *bunk*]: Shhh! She'll hear you and—*pounce!*

Jake [*amused*]: What's the matter with her?

Liz: Says she's got a headache, but it ain't. No, siree. A broken nose, that's what it is—out of joint because Velma's *It* now instead uh her. No more presents or letters—except from that durned fool Admirer——

Jake: A slick guy for free advertisin'!

Liz: Papers, Mrs. Morton, ever'body makin' over Velma, and *she* won't even help her dress or wish her good luck. Mean, that's what she is—just like my jury. 'Cause I wanted 'em to hang me, they wouldn't. Spite work, that's what it was.

Jake: Never mind, you can appeal.

Liz [*straightens up*]: And go through another trial? Not much I don't! I didn't mind goin' over *once*—the lawyers and judge has got to have somethin' to do and I don't mind helpin' 'em once, but I ain't got time for such foolishness again. The folks likes their fun and I done *my* part, [*smiles in pleased recollection*] didn't I?

Jake [*also smiles*]: You *certainly* did!

Liz: My lawyer had me talk to show 'em I was crazy, but I fooled him, all right, didn't I? [*Begins rocking and sobbing and wailing.*]

Roxie [*sharply, opening door*]: Shut up, Liz, you're makin' my head worse.

Liz: Glad of it. Hope it busts.

[*A shoe sails by,* ROXIE *limps out to retrieve it, and becomes angelic at the sight of* JAKE.]

ROXIE: Why, Mr. Callahan!

JAKE: Hello, Carrots!

LIZ: Go 'way, he's mine! He's havin' an interview with me—[*to* JAKE] *ain't* you. [*Tries to push* ROXIE *back with her soapy hands;* ROXIE *administers a good sharp slap, and* LIZ *cries.*]

ROXIE: Hush! or I'll tell God on you!

LIZ [*muttering*]: Go on and tell! You're such an old liar He won't believe you. [*Returns to scrubbing.*]

ROXIE [*sweetly to* JAKE]: O Mr. Callahan, I'm so glad it's you! You've been so kind to me—so—so—mag-nani*mous*——

LIZ: Says that to all of 'em—don't you believe her.

ROXIE [*soulfully, to* JAKE]: And now I'm goin' to do somethin' for you; it's a story.

JAKE: All right, spill it.

ROXIE [*wearily*]: I can't sleep—my head hurts! I've had a terrible night! Tossed and wept, sobbed re-morse——

JAKE [*gets up in disgust*]: O my God, don't start that again! Nobody gives a damn how you're sleeping.

ROXIE [*shrilly*]: They do too! Don't you remem-ber . . . [*Follows him.*]

JAKE: Sure, *once*—when the story was new, but it's dead now. You'll have to pull a better line than that.

ROXIE [*with sudden inspiration*]: *I've* got it: a scoop for you—a front-page story!

JAKE [*skeptically*]: Yeah?

ROXIE: It's a dress—you can raffle it off—sell chances on it . . . [*takes* VELMA'S *green dress from the box; he shakes his head in rejection and she goes on with inspiration*] . . . The dress I wore the first time I ever went wrong!

JAKE: O my God! [*Backs away from her.*]

ROXIE: It's a museum piece. [*Follows him.*]

JAKE: Then put it back in the case.

ROXIE [*dangerously*]: I'll give it to another paper.

JAKE: Just try it, you little publicity hound! You've sure got it bad. Now listen: You'll have another fling at front page when your trial starts, but until then there's not a chance in the world! For they've caught Kitty Baxter!

ROXIE: O my God, *another* one!

JAKE: And she's got you faded, Roxie. She's a Tiger Cat and you're just a little white kitten. But I will do this: use you in a picture with her: "The Jazz-Slayer Meets the Bandit Queen."

ROXIE: Nothing doing!

JAKE: Whole cheese or none, huh? Well, suit yourself. But if you can't play ball, you'd better curl up [*nods toward cell*] and go to sleep for the next four months.

ROXIE [*genuinely startled*]: Four months! It ain't goin' to take *that* long!

JAKE: Sure! The September calendar—maybe October. Billy goes abroad for July and August.

ROXIE: *What!* Hoofs it to Europe on *my money*—the clothes I sold off of my back to pay him? And I stay cooped up here! [*Her eyes flash.*] Do you think I'm goin' to stand for that?

JAKE [*calmly*]: Sure. What can you do about it?

ROXIE [*determinedly*]: I don't know, but . . . [*Taps foot, thinking.*] God damn it, and I got my clothes all planned for a summer trial!

[*The bell rings. Moans and wails are heard*

from MAGGIE *at the end of the screen, and out of sympathy* LIZ *starts up also.*]

SUNSHINE [*comes in and stops in chagrin at sight of* JAKE]: O dear!

JAKE [*grins*]: I beat you—but we're both early.

ROXIE [*goes to her, confidentially*]: O Miss Sunshine, I've something *very* important to tell you, something——

SUNSHINE [*slips out of her grasp with a sweet smile*]: Later, my dear. I've a message for Velma first. [*Goes on upstairs.*]

    [*In the meantime* MATRON *has herded* MAGGIE *and her visitors, dimly seen through the screen, down toward the elevator.*]

MAGGIE [*weeping—great sobs and wails*]: Mine baby! Mine baby! Gif her to me!

MATRON [*grasps her arm and tries to draw her away*]: Shut up, you!

MAGGIE [*clings to screen with both hands*]: Let me see her—chust let me *see* her—*vonce* . . .

MATRON: Shut up! You can't see her—do you hear? [*To man outside.*] Go on away—your time's up. [*To elevator man.*] Take 'em on down, Tom.

MAGGIE: *Vonce*—let me *hold* her. . . . [*Runs along the screen like an animal and gives a final piercing wail as the elevator clicks.*]

MATRON: That's enough out of you now. Your baby's *gone,* do you understand, *gone.*

JAKE: What's the row? Who's she?

MATRON: Moonshine Maggie.

JAKE: Oh, the hunyak they nabbed for sellin' booze.

MATRON: Get her to tell you about it—she's a scream. Maggie, come here. . . . [*Woman comes slowly.*]

What's the matter, Maggie? Why don't you go *with* your baby?

MAGGIE [*simply, looking up through her tears*]: They won't let me.

MATRON: *Who* won't let you?

MAGGIE: Uncle Sam. [*Crying again.*] O missus, please, missus——

MATRON: Here, wait a minute. *Why* won't he let you? You killed a man, that's why. You're a bad girl. [*To* JAKE, *in enjoyment.*] She always cries at that. [*To* MAGGIE, *encouragingly.*] Come on tell us about it. [*Pointing to* JAKE, *with a burst of inspiration.*] Here's your Uncle Sam now!

MAGGIE [*peers through fingers at* JAKE]: You my Uncle Sam?

MATRON [*pleased with her genius*]: Sure. And he can help you if you just——

MAGGIE [*flings herself on knees before* JAKE *in wild earnestness*]: O mister, mister, Uncle Sam, let me go! My baby *need* me—Maggie not bad——

MATRON: Wait a minute; why did you kill him, Maggie?

    [ROXIE, *perched on the table, smoking, watches thoughtfully the scene that follows.*]

MAGGIE [*clasps her hands on* JAKE'S *knees and her eyes search his*]: Me not kill him, mister. [*Pulls the words out, one by one, and gestures.*] He come to our house —mine husband, me, mine baby—two months old she was—a *little* baby . . . [*Sobs.*]

MATRON: Forget the kid—go on.

JAKE [*gently*]: Who came, Maggie?

MAGGIE: Johann—*him.* Christmas Eve——

JAKE [*to* MATRON]: This Christmas?

MATRON: A year ago—been waitin' trial.

JAKE [*To* ROXIE]: See? And you a-growlin' over four
months!
[*She tosses her head.*]
MAGGIE: An' he say, "Gimme drink, Maggie." And I
give him. An' he drink, I drink, mine husband—all,
[*grows distressed*] an' next day . . . men come—
men come for *me,* an' say *I* kill him—*me!* [*Beats
her breast and sobs again.*]
MATRON: Found him dead in a ditch—too much moonshine.
JAKE [*soberly*]: Gotta know your bootlegger these
days!
MAGGIE: An' they took me away—an' I not see mine
baby chust there . . . [*Points to screen.*] O Uncle
Sam, mine baby need me!
MATRON: Funny, ain't it, the way she takes on over
that kid!
JAKE: Did they use it at the trial? [MATRON *shakes her
head.*] Lord, what rotten management!
MAGGIE: O mister, please, give me mine baby! [*Starts
sobbing and wailing.*]
MATRON [*takes her arm*]: That's enough now. You
can't have your baby. You're a bad girl. [*Starts her
to the stairs.*]
MAGGIE [*shrieks*]: But mine baby!
MATRON: Shut up! Nobody cares about you or your
baby! [*Follows her up the stairs.*]
JAKE [*soberly*]: Yep: nobody cares!
LIZ [*bursts into shrill laughter*]: It's 'cause we ain't got
bobbed hair and wear cotton stockin's, Maggie, that's
what it is!
[*Bell rings and* MATRON *answers.*]
ROXIE: What do you reckon a jury thinks about?
LIZ: Juries don't think—they acts.

ROXIE: But what counts *most?*

JAKE: Just being a woman!

ROXIE: Yeah—look at Maggie.

JAKE: That wasn't the jury's fault; she had a bum lawyer. . . . D'yuh remember the Harland case? She fed lysol to her two stepchildren and the baby died; then the last day of the trial they had the other one run down the aisle cryin' "Mama! Mama!" and the jury sent her home to her husband and the dear little one who needed her! . . . And now this hunyak— a decent lawyer with a sob like that would had the jury wipin' its eyes and givin' her a medal. Gee, it gets me: wastin' a kid that way! [*Shakes his head regretfully as he saunters down the corridor.*]

VOICES [*upstairs*]: Good luck, Velma! Happy days! By-by, Old Timer!

VELMA [*enters, followed by* SUNSHINE, *in beige coatdress, with slip-on gloves, scarlet gardenia, carrying a blue dress*]: . . . and we sail the sixteenth, if— everything comes out all right . . . [*To* MATRON, *holding up blue dress.*] I'm taking the blue, so if he don't like this I can change! [*Goes to make-up box.*] Just a little more color: beige is so trying. [*Carefully adds rouge.*]

MATRON: You better hurry—the bailiff's waitin'.

VELMA [*with genuine tragedy*]: My God, the lipstick's gone! [*The* MATRON *dashes to her—they search frantically.*] Yes, it is—*gone!*

SUNSHINE: Here, take mine!

VELMA [*reaches for it eagerly, then sinks in despair*]: But it's rose and I need tangerine!

VELMA [*Clasps her hand to her head in frenzy*]: God, I can *never* face the jury *now!* [*Staggers to the door.*]

MATRON: Well, yuh gotta go anyway.

ROXIE [*grabs* SUNSHINE *as she tries to follow* VELMA]: O Miss Sunshine, I've got a scoop for you: it's a letter from the guy who bought my garters and he's goin' on a hunger strike until I'm freed.

[SUNSHINE *tries to pull away.* ROXIE *lowers her tone mysteriously.*]

And I've got a package—a dress—and I want you to send it back and tell him it ain't refined to take clothes from men!

[*There's a noise in the hall—the sound of scuffling, muffled oaths, and a husky voice snarls:* "You God-damned bums!"]

[SUNSHINE *rushes away, leaving* ROXIE *alone in the middle of the floor. She stamps her foot and once more retires to her cell in rage.*]

MATRON [*at door*]: No, you needn't. And if she tries any bitin' *here,* I'll have 'em pull ever' tooth in her head!

[*Enter the* BAXTER GIRL, *a wiry young tough with insolent eyes set deep in a thin white face, square hard jaw, and straight scarlet mouth now drawn tight. She wears a rough topcoat over sweater and skirt, and a velvet tam over a matted curly bob.*

[*There's a moment's silence as she saunters to the middle of the floor and takes in the room: the white walls, the bunks,* LIZ *kneeling like a statue,* SUNSHINE *quivering with excitement,* JAKE *slouched against the wall, the* MATRON *watchful and waiting.*]

KITTY: Humph. [*She swings herself up on the table, takes off her hat and runs grimy hand through grimier head.*]

SUNSHINE [*tremulously*]: O Miss Baxter . . . [KITTY

turns.] I—I'm from the *Evening Star*—Mary Sunshine from the *Evening Star* . . . [*Falters under* KITTY'*s gaze.*] . . . and we'd like for you to —everyone is so *interested*—I wonder if you'd mind saying just a word or two?

KITTY [*agreeably*]: Sure: I'll say three: go to hell.

SUNSHINE: O dear! O *dear!*

MATRON [*severely*]: Now, look here, Kitty, that's no way to talk. The young lady——

KITTY [*impatiently, to* JAKE]: Get into this. I can't fight with old women, and I eat children like her— [*nods toward* SUNSHINE] for breakfast. What's on your chest? Spit it out.

JAKE: Do you remember me?

KITTY [*shakes head, flippantly*]: I've seen so many handsome faces in the last two days . . .

JAKE [*quietly*]: I was at the show-up when Mickey pointed you out.

KITTY [*eagerly*]: You were? What did he say when I'd gone—tell me! [*Goes into a rage.*] *Damn* him! If it wasn't for him—the dirty squealer!—I wouldn't be here!

SUNSHINE [*tremulously*]: O Miss Baxter, are you— are you—sorry?

KITTY: You little fool! Of course I'm sorry. Who wants to get caught? And I'd made my getaway if——

JAKE: Pretty slick.

KITTY: Wasn't it though! Passed three cops! And if I hadn't waited for *him* . . . [*Turns her back and when she faces them again her face is wet with tears of rage.*] O women are *fools!*

MATRON [*sympathetically*]: I never knew a killin' yet that a man wasn't back of it.

JAKE [*easily*]: And this other guy——

KITTY [*swiftly*]: What other guy?

JAKE [*with a knowing look*]: Say, don't you think we know?

KITTY: I know damn well you don't.

JAKE: Don't you think Mickey told me?

KITTY: Mickey don't *know*. God and me are the only ones: and we don't tell.

JAKE: It would help your case.

SUNSHINE: Yes, indeed, Miss Baxter.

KITTY: I've heard that line for two days, now, and get this: I don't squeal. They'll send me up, I guess— maybe, I'll swing—but I'll die like a lady!

JAKE [*heartily*]: Atta boy, Kitty!

SUNSHINE [*hurriedly*]: O you won't—er—*swing*. Women never—*swing*.

KITTY: Say, I wear skirts but I got guts, and I don't yell "King's X" when I'm caught. And I'll get mine, all right! Yuh see, I didn't just *kill* a man—what's a little murder! But this was a stick-up—would yuh believe it: an Ingersoll watch and four dollars! And the man—accidental-like—got bumped off. O yes, they'll get me! You can poison your husband or shoot your lover, but the pocket-book hits 'em where they live. Even a juryman has four dollars and an Ingersoll, and that makes me a "dangerous woman" . . . Think of it—me, Kitty—[*slumps in dejection*] caught on a job like that!

SUNSHINE: How long have you—er—been banditing?

KITTY: Say, for the last ten years I've carried a gun where most girls carry a powder-puff. [*Flippantly.*] A direct descendant of Captain KIDD.

[ROXIE *opens the door*, KITTY *turns, and the*

two stare at each other in instant and thorough hatred.]

What about you, Angel Face, don't you want in on this?

JAKE: That's Roxie Hart, Kitty.

KITTY: And who the hell is she?

MATRON [*proudly*]: The prettiest one we've ever had!

KITTY: My God, what is this: a *beauty* contest?

JAKE: You've read about her.

KITTY [*coolly*]: I don't read news—I make it.

ROXIE [*flares*]: So do I! A damn sight more than *you* ever will!

KITTY: O is *that* so!

ROXIE: Yes, *that's* so. Thirty-five columns and twenty-two pictures.

KITTY: Hell, what's that? If I told all *I* know, it would make a dictionary, [*to reporters*] wouldn't it!

SUNSHINE [*afraid to breathe*]: O *yes*, Miss Baxter! It's so—so significant of this age—youth and jazz and the quest for——

KITTY: Shut up!! . . . [*To* JAKE.] What's her racket anyway?

ROXIE [*on verge of raging tears*]: *You* know what I did!

SUNSHINE [*trembling*]: A man—another man——

KITTY: O yes—your sweetie: "Killed him rather than lose him" . . . *I* remember. Say that's old stuff. [*To* ROXIE.] Move on, sister, you're dead and don't know it.·

ROXIE [*screaming*]: I am not dead—I'll show you! [*She grabs* KITTY's *hair, all ready for a grand feminine fight, but the* TIGER GIRL *tosses her off; she starts back for more, but the* MATRON *interferes.*]

MATRON: Now, Roxie! [*Gives her a push that sends her spinning toward her cell;* ROXIE *spits like a kitten at her enemy, who triumphantly seats herself on the table.*]

KITTY: What's her record anyway? Watch me bust it.

JAKE [*to* KITTY]: Shoot the works, kid.

[ROXIE *paces up and down in thought and rage as* SUNSHINE *and* JAKE *cluster around* KITTY.]

SUNSHINE: Tell us *just* how you happened to start! What were the factors in your life that caused you to—er—take it up? Was it jazz? The thirst for excitement? The quest for adventure? Are you a thrill-slayer?

[*Unable to endure it any longer* ROXIE *gives a sudden shriek and crumbles in a faint. The* MATRON, SUNSHINE *and* JAKE *wheel from* KITTY; LIZ *stops scrubbing and sits up like a squirrel;* KITTY, *from the table, watches in disgust.*]

JAKE: Good Lord!

SUNSHINE: O what is it! She's fainted!

MATRON: My God, on top of everything else! [*They all rush and kneel beside her.*] Water!

LIZ: Water! Water! [*She rushes over with her bucket of suds and is intensely disappointed when* JAKE *prevents the administration of her aid.*]

SUNSHINE: Has she been sick?

JAKE [*to* MATRON]: Shall I get the doctor?

KITTY [*contemptuously from her perch*]: Ain't that just like a woman?

ROXIE [*moans with eyes still closed*]: O dear. . . . O dear. . . . Oh . . .

MATRON [*bathes her head briskly*]: There, there!

[ROXIE *opens her eyes and smiles wanly.*]

ROXIE [*weakly and sweetly—little Eva en route to heaven*]: I'm all right. . . . Don't worry . . . about—*me*. . . .

MATRON: She's comin' around all right now. . . . [*To ROXIE, who tries to sit up.*] Aren't you ashamed to——

ROXIE [*sinks back gasping*]: I can't *breathe*. . . .

MATRON: Here, help me with her.

JAKE [*nods toward the cell*]: In there?

MATRON [*shakes her head*]: No! On the table—air . . .

[SUNSHINE *gets a pillow from the cell and brushes* KITTY *aside to make room for the improvised cot.*]

Look out! [JAKE *lifts the drooped body.*] There! [*To* KITTY, *impatiently.*] Clear on out—upstairs— show her, Liz.

[KITTY *follows* LIZ *in swaggering silence, and the* MATRON *disappears for camphor and ammonia;* SUNSHINE *and* JAKE *stand looking down at* ROXIE.]

ROXIE [*revives a little, crying*]: O dear . . . dear . . . I can't *bear* it! [*Her slender frame shakes with sobs.*]

SUNSHINE: Bear *what*, darling—*tell* me!

ROXIE: Go 'way—let me alone! [*Sobbing more heartily.*] Here in jail— O dear, my . . . baby . . .

[*The* MATRON *returns on this word and there's grand astonishment all around.*]

SUNSHINE: *Baby!*

ROXIE [*faintly, wanly*]: . . . when my child . . . is born . . .

JAKE [*in genuine alarm*]: Good *God!* Say, I *must* get the doctor!

MATRON [*applies smelling salts, ammonia, etc.*]: I

knew she wasn't well, but I never dreamt *this*. . . .

SUNSHINE [*in hushed ecstasy*]: Isn't it too divine! "Stork Hovers over County Jail." [*To* JAKE.] Could you ask for anything better?

JAKE [*dubiously*]: No-o . . . just so it don't light right *now*.

SUNSHINE [*superiorly*]: Don't be silly . . . it won't.

JAKE: How do you know?

SUNSHINE: No such luck.

MATRON [*with sudden inspiration*]: *That's* why she wanted her lawyer!

JAKE [*revives*]: Gosh—it's a whale of a story! Think what it will do to her case! "Young Mother Awaits Trial"——

SUNSHINE [*corrects*]: "*Girl* Mother Awaits Trial"— isn't it *too* wonderful! [*To* MATRON.] Was one ever born here before?

MATRON [*shakes head*]: Not in my day.

[*The bell rings and she goes to answer;* ROXIE *tries to sit up.*]

SUNSHINE [*tenderly*]: No, no, darling, lie still! [*Adjusts her pillow.*]

ROXIE [*faintly and sweetly*]: I don't . . . want to . . . *bother* you. . . .

SUNSHINE [*purrs*]: *Dear* Mrs. Hart . . . tell Sunshine—tell Sunshine *all!*

JAKE [*awkwardly*]: Feeling better?

ROXIE [*in hollow voice*]: O yes. . . . *I'm* all right. . . . [*Sinks back exhausted to disprove words.*]

[MATRON *admits* MR. FLYNN, *who tries to conceal his perturbation over what the* MATRON *has evidently told him.*]

SUNSHINE [*skips to meet him*]: O Mr. Flynn, isn't it too *marvelous!*

JAKE: It's a knockout, isn't it!

FLYNN: What's this, young lady? Why didn't you let me know?

ROXIE [*looks up sweetly*]: I did try to, but you wouldn't come.

FLYNN: Umm, yes . . . I was busy. Well, well, it's all right now.

ROXIE [*with sweet bitterness*]: "All right?"

SUNSHINE [*hops up and down*]: Isn't it gorgeous? Aren't you *glad?*

ROXIE: "Glad?" Oh! [*Gives a moan.*] To have your baby born—*here?* [*They all look at each other startled.*]

SUNSHINE: Wonderful! I'll phone all the women's clubs, the Parent-Teachers, the Civic League! We'll ask for letters: "Shall an Innocent Child Bear the Stigma of Jail?"

JAKE: They'll eat it alive!

FLYNN [*to* SUNSHINE]: Good! And then a petition——

SUNSHINE: O yes, miles and miles of names!

FLYNN: —asking that bail be granted so that an innocent babe can be born in God's great outdoors! [*His arm sweeps the Western hemisphere.*]

JAKE: But you won't wait for *that,* will you? When——?

SUNSHINE: When is it to be?

ROXIE: Oh—! [*Closes her eyes a moment.*] Not till fall—September.

FLYNN: Umm . . . then I'd better crowd it in before I sail—yes, I'll rush it to the jury in June.

     [*A look of triumph flashes over* ROXIE's *face as she sinks back on the pillow.*]

SUNSHINE: What jury would condemn a mother-to-be!

JAKE: And, Billy, *could* a jury condemn her to death, or would it be passing judgment on two lives instead of one? And if they did, could the sentence be executed, or——

FLYNN: See the State's Attorney on that. [*Chuckles.*] It's a solar plexus for him, all right!

ROXIE [*sits up dramatically*]: My *own* life doesn't matter, but that of my child! . . . [*Gives a little tremolo as she sinks back*] . . . my child . . .

FLYNN: Don't worry, my dear: the American public will fight to the death for your innocent unborn babe!

SUNSHINE: And every true woman! Why, Motherhood itself is at stake, *isn't* it, Mr. Flynn? O wouldn't it be *wonderful* if the trial could come just before Mother's Day!

ROXIE [*soulfully*]: You've been so kind to me, Miss Sunshine . . . If it's a girl, I'm goin' to name it after you!

SUNSHINE [*kisses her*]: You darling . . . that's just too *sweet* . . .

ROXIE [*takes Jake's hand and looks up fondly at him*]: And if it's a boy, after *you*.

JAKE [*beams fatuously, holds her hand a moment, then drops it like a hot cake*]: *Hell,* no! I'm married, *happily* married, and aim to stay that way. Thanks— thanks—but . . . [*Backs off.*] Slip it to Billy here.

FLYNN [*also in alarm as she looks up at him*]: O no— *no.* I appreciate the honor, but——

JAKE: A first son should always be named for his father. [*Slowly, slowly his expression changes.*] *Say* —who *is* papa?

FLYNN [*simulating indignation*]: *What!* I'm ashamed of you, Jake! *Ashamed!*

JAKE [*slaps him on back*]: Take it easy! I mean Casely or Hart!

FLYNN: To think you'd insult this brave little woman!

JAKE: Insult or not, it's what they're all going to be askin'.

FLYNN [*steps toward him in pretended rage*]: Callahan, get out! I don't want to talk to you! Get *out!*

MATRON [*sings out at door*]: Your husband, Mrs. Hart!

JAKE [*grins and goes*]: *That's* the bird *I* want to see!
    [MARY SUNSHINE *and* JAKE *scurry to the door.*]

FLYNN [*fiercely to* ROXIE, *who half rises from her couch*]: You little *fool!* Who *is* the father anyway?

ROXIE [*shrugs her shoulders wisely*]: Don't worry: he'll stick.

FLYNN: I don't want him to! [*Bitterly.*] It'll make you look as black as hell! All the sympathy for *him!*

ROXIE: I can handle him all right!

FLYNN: Shut up! You've done enough! I've got to make him *divorce* you!

ROXIE [*sits up alert*]: Alimony! [*Falls back as* AMOS *enters, with hat on back of his head and fatuous grin.* JAKE *saunters on one side,* SUNSHINE *skips on the other, and the* MATRON *trails after them.*]

AMOS [*genially to* FLYNN, *who comes to meet him*]: Well, I guess the cigars are on me!

FLYNN [*slaps him on the back*]: That's the way to take it, Hart—be a sport; what do *you* care if people laugh!

AMOS [*blankly, losing a little hilarity*]: "Laugh?"

FLYNN: After all, people's jokes . . .

JAKE [*suddenly*]: By God, it *is* funny!
    [*They've reached the couch:* AMOS *tiptoes in*

*awe and looks down at the heaving figure, face
hidden by her arm.*]

AMOS [*in awed whisper*]: Will she—know me?

JAKE [*gives a howl of merriment*]: O my God! She
ain't havin' it *now!*

SUNSHINE: O Mr. Hart, not till fall—September . . .
[*There is a pause; AMOS stands, eyes cast to-
ward ceiling, lost in calculation. JAKE lifts his
hand with a knowing look toward FLYNN. SUN-
SHINE gives a gasp.*]
O Mr. Hart, you don't mean——!

AMOS [*holds up hand to stop her*]: Wait a minute. . . .
[*Finishes calculation.*] Say, you don't put nothin'
over on me!

SUNSHINE [*in ecstasy over possible new turn*]: Lovely,
lovely. . . .

FLYNN [*in melancholy tone*]: My client needs your
support, Mr. Hart.

AMOS [*bitterly*]: Yeah—"Meal Ticket"—that's all
I've ever been! Say, you can't make a fool out of
me!

JAKE: What are you goin' to do—divorce her?

AMOS [*loftily*]: I ain't sayin' *what* I'll do! [*Starts off
but stops as BABE is admitted with camera.*]

JAKE: O Babe, a couple uh flashes here!

BABE [*backs off from ROXIE and makes for the stairs*]:
Not that lens-louse—I'm after the Tiger Girl!

JAKE: It's a scoop, kid, come on! [*With a grand gesture toward ROXIE.*] Waitin' the stork: a baby!

BABE [*to AMOS, as he sets up camera*]: Well, Court-
Plaster, you in on this?

FLYNN [*doesn't give him a chance to answer*]: No!
He's cast her off, forsaken her!

AMOS: Wait till I see my lawyer. I ain't as dumb as

I look! September—hell! [*Goes off grandly.*]

ROXIE: Amos! My husband! [*Through tears, with out-stretched arms to* AMOS—*when she's sure he's gone.*] Deserted in my hour of need!

BABE: Look at the camera, sweetheart!

ROXIE: Wait a minute. [*To* SUNSHINE.] My sewing.

[SUNSHINE *hands her the baby dress left by* MAGGIE *in the rocking-chair. She bends over the dress in sewing posture, then turns Madonna face to the camera.*]

I'm making every stitch myself.

FLYNN [*takes pose by her side*]: Deserted wife and mother!

JAKE: Hot stuff!

BABE: Hold it!

[*Flash, bang,* CURTAIN!]

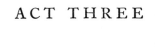

ACT THREE

ACT III

Scene i

*Seven weeks later, a morning in June. The prisoner's
room before Court opens.*

*A small room, dingy and bare, with great high brown
walls that are beginning to scale off. A door at the
right leads to the Bridge of Sighs, a window at the
left looks upon air shaft and gray brick wall, and a
center door opens into a small vestibule through
which may be seen two other doors: one directly opposite, leading to the jury room, and one at the
right, to the courtroom.*

*A long bare table, half a dozen straight chairs, and a
bleary mirror constitute the furnishings. Flowers are
stacked on the table, dresses thrown over a chair in
the corner, the make-up box is open—it looks like the
dressing-room of a star.*

*The prisoner's bailiff sits by the door, sleeping in tilted
chair. Now and then it drops to the floor with a thud,
but he quickly rights it and resumes his dream.*

Roxie *sits in a chair at left of table—turned relatively
as it will be the witness-stand in the following scene.
She wears a dress with meaning: heavy white crepe
with surplice collar and bishop sleeves—a nun would
envy its chastity; white shoes and hose of perplexing
nudity. Her feet are crossed carelessly and one lily
hand dangles a cigarette. Her eyes, wide and inno-*

cent, stare soulfully at the blank wall that represents the jury.

FLYNN *paces up and down at the right, coaching from the sidelines.*

ROXIE: . . . "my innocent unborn babe. . . ."

FLYNN: Throw your head back—*nobly!* [*She does.*] That's right!—wait! Don't look at the jury on that —you forget them—seek the eyes of your husband. He'll be over here. . . .

ROXIE: "He's divorced me, cast me off,"—I got that all right!—"but still the father of my child!"

FLYNN [*with deep emotion*]: And the man you really love! . . . Once the jury get *that* and the fact he wants you *back*, why, they'll fall all over themselves to play Cupid and restore you to his arms!

ROXIE [*studies vanity-case and adjusts make-up*]: All right; where do we go from here: . . . "my innocent unborn babe . . . ?"

FLYNN: That's all—you've finished your story: the plain, unvarnished statement of a simple, God-fearing working-girl. Sure you've got it?

ROXIE: *Got* it? I could say it in my sleep!

FLYNN: Then the cross-examination——

ROXIE: He'd better watch his step, that Harrison! If he calls me names—like he did yesterday——

FLYNN: You cry.

ROXIE: I'll crown him!

FLYNN: No, you *won't*. God, if that jury ever saw you in action—! Remember: no matter what he *says* or how mad he gets, you shrink—and cower—[*illustrates, she imitates*]—and cry, till the jury are ready to knock him down! [*Grins.*] They always lose when they bulldoze a woman! And if he says they didn't use physical violence to get those confessions——

ROXIE [*with alacrity*]: I'll hold out my arm for you to see the marks! [*Does so.*]

FLYNN: Right. And when you answer him: "I don't know. . . ." "I don't remember. . . ." [*Acts part for her.*] Weak, faint, frightened—always to the jury—with a little flutter—[*blinks his eyes appealingly, she imitates*]—especially that twenty-minute egg in the corner.

ROXIE [*rises, saunters to large mirror*]: Say, you don't have to tell me how to handle *them* babies! I ain't watched them three days for nothin'! [*Darkly.*] I've done ever'thing but give 'em my phone number!

FLYNN [*laughs coarsely*]: That'll come later. Beautiful work.

ROXIE [*with languid complacence*]: Technique: I got it.
[*There's a quick knock at the door:* SUNSHINE *with an armful of flowers;* JAKE *lounges on the threshold; through the open door a glimpse of the courtroom noise and confusion.* FLYNN *joins* JAKE, SUNSHINE *crosses to* ROXIE.]

SUNSHINE: *Good*-morning! And how is she today? [*Gives her the flowers.*] From the Parent-Teachers!

ROXIE [*tremulous voice*]: Lovely . . . it's kind friends like these . . . [*Overcome with emotion.*]

SUNSHINE [*triumphantly*]: And another baby carriage, dear! That's five!
[ROXIE *involuntarily shudders; places flowers with others.*]

JAKE [*in doorway, to* FLYNN]: Biggest crowd since Loeb and Leopold! Get ready to strut your stuff, Billy!

Voice of BABE [*outside*]: Come on, Billy, if you want in on this picture!

[FLYNN *goes;* ROXIE *gives a slide across the room, but* JAKE *bars her.*]

JAKE: That ain't your cue: men only this time, sweetheart, I'll call you when the stage is set. [*Closes door after him.*]

SUNSHINE [*who's been fluttering over letters and wires on table*]: Any more proposals?

ROXIE: O yes. . . . A beautiful one from a New York millionaire who wants to adopt me . . . and one from a widower in Colorado. . . . [*Hands her the letter.*]

SUNSHINE: "A chance to forget . . . and a name for your fatherless child. . . ." Do you think you could ever——?

ROXIE [*leans back, wan and pale*]: It's hard . . . all alone . . . but [*shakes her head sadly*] I can only love once. . . . [*Her lip trembles, on the verge of tears.*]

SUNSHINE [*pats her hand*]: *Dear* Mrs. Hart! [*To* FLYNN, *who returns.*] Isn't it *wonderful* the way she bears up?

FLYNN [*gravely*]: We must let her rest now—a terrible strain! You understand. . . . [SUNSHINE *nods and goes,* ROXIE *revives, and* FLYNN *takes papers from brief case and runs through them.*] Better go on with my plea before Judge gets here . . . Let's see, where were we. . . .

ROXIE [*resumes seat that represents the witness-stand* —FLYNN *sits at the table, across from her*]: You'd told how they rushed in that night and found me in my kimona. . . .

FLYNN: Ummm . . . got to cut this some if we finish today.

ROXIE: *Today?*

FLYNN: To the jury by eight and a verdict by ten—
that'll catch "the home."

ROXIE: But maybe Harrison——

FLYNN: We've just agreed: three hours for him and
three for me. . . .

ROXIE: But *me*——!

FLYNN: O it won't take long for you!

ROXIE [*softly, as her eyes narrow*—FLYNN, *writing,
does not see*]: I hope not. [*Sigh; pause; burst of
confidence.*] But I'm so *worried.*

FLYNN: Nonsense! When they hear my *speech* . . .

ROXIE: But, Mr. Flynn . . . this dress. . . .

FLYNN [*looks up startled*]: Dress?

ROXIE: If you finish tonight—I can't walk out of here
all in *white!*

FLYNN: Nonsense!

ROXIE: If I only had a coat . . . You've been so particular about my clothes. . . .

FLYNN: I don't give a damn if you wear gunny-sack
after the verdict.

ROXIE: I wish *I* could feel that way. O dear, I hope I
can keep my *mind* on his questions.

FLYNN: You will. All right now, snap into this: He will
ask——

ROXIE: And I do hope I don't get tangled up and forget—there's so much to remember! That would be
awful, wouldn't it?—all on account of a silly old
coat—or a cape, maybe—that wouldn't cost over a
hundred dollars!

FLYNN [*stares in exasperation, then dawning compre-
hension: reaches for his purse and counts out the
money*]: You've learned a great deal in three months,
my dear.

ROXIE [*puts money in envelope with note*]: Thank

you, *dear* Mr. Flynn! [*Gives envelope to bailiff.*] Miss Sunshine, please. [*He goes; she drops the languid pose and turns to* FLYNN *with a hearty grin.*] Atta boy, let's go!

FLYNN [*returns to brief*]: He'll ask you why you didn't tell them the story you told this morning. . . .

ROXIE: Yeah, I've wondered about that, too.

FLYNN: You droop your head. . . . "Let us think: when and to whom did she finally reveal the dearest secret of a woman's heart? Only after long gray days in jail when her soul cried out for sympathy. . . ." Then I'll point to Mary Sunshine . . . "to a *woman*. And the State's Attorney wonders why she didn't confide in him!" And you look modest.

ROXIE: Still droopin'?

FLYNN [*nods*]: "They threatened and tortured and were successful in tearing from her the confession of her weakness——"

ROXIE: What do I do?

FLYNN [*waves for silence*]: —"the frailty that is woman in loving too well, but she kept locked within the sanctuary of her heart"——[ROXIE, *on her own initiative, tries to follow with effective pantomime*] —"the sacred secret of her coming motherhood." [*Looks up and catches her in ludicrous pose.*] What the hell——

ROXIE [*with dignity*]: I'm only trying to do what you *say*.

FLYNN [*grimly*]: We're not playing charades. Droop, that's all you do: *droop*. . . . Then I turn toward you: "I'm thankful! I'm glad! I'm *proud* that you did, Roxie Hart!"

ROXIE [*lifts head expectantly*]: Then what do *I* do?

FLYNN [*glares at her*]: What do you *want* to do—turn a cart-wheel?

ROXIE [*rebelliously*]: Looks kinda dumb just to *sit* there.

FLYNN: I'll take care of that. You *droop* and that's all. [*She tosses her head unconvinced as he skims on down the page.*] Ummm . . . "sorry" . . . "sorry" . . . ummm . . . here we are! "If sorrow could avail, Fred Casely would be here now, for she'd give her life and gladly, to bring the dead man back." You nod. [*She does, raptly.*] "But we can't do that, gentlemen. You may take her life as the State asks, but it won't bring Casely back. . . ." That's always news to 'em. . . . *Now* . . . *Now* . . . *Here's* where you start to cry. [*Covers his face completely with his hands in demonstration.*]

ROXIE [*sarcastically*]: Why don't you get me a mask?

FLYNN: Softly, very softly. . . . [*Orchestral gesture.*] "And for what purpose? To protect society? Do you fear that weeping girl?" [*Meets* ROXIE's *glare of cold suspicion.*] Weep, you fool! Can't you see how damned silly——

ROXIE [*hastily takes handkerchief*]: O yes, I was so interested I forgot.

FLYNN: Weep! "For her reformation?" Long speech ending: "We can't give her happiness—" you lift your head and listen through a mist of tears—[*she does*]—"no, it is too late for that. Betrayed, crushed, we can let her pick up the broken fragments of life, the tangled threads—" quiver your lip! . . . "We can give her another *chance!*" And that's all for *you.*

ROXIE: All for *me?* What's the rest of it about?

FLYNN [*with satisfaction*]: Harrison.

ROXIE: What's *he* got to do with it?

FLYNN: I show it ain't justice he wants, but conviction. For *that* means promotion.

ROXIE: And how long will that take?

FLYNN [*carelessly*]: Oh, an hour or so.

ROXIE [*aghast*]: An *hour* or so—talkin' about *him?* What's the big idea?

FLYNN: Why, it gets their minds off of you.

ROXIE: O it does, does it!

FLYNN: And gets them thinkin' what a dirty crook *he* is!

ROXIE: Say, whose trial is this: mine or Harrison's?

FLYNN [*chuckles as he takes a cigar*]: His, before I get through! And don't I crucify him!

ROXIE [*drums her fingers ominously on the table, seething*]: And where do *I* come in? What do I do?

FLYNN [*roaring*]: My God, is this a circus? Sit still, that's what you do, and look downcast and sad—far off, not at the jury—or bury your head in your arms on the table——

ROXIE [*bangs her hand down on the table*]: Like hell I do. It's *me* they want to see! Not *you,* hoppin' around like a little fat monkey!

FLYNN [*purple*]: It's my *speech* that brings 'em— good God, they've had enough of your damned face! And it's my speech that'll save your neck— [*significantly*] if it's saved. [*They stand glaring at each other, and* ROXIE *yields sulkily.*]

ROXIE: Aw right, go ahead and *talk* then. But not about Harrison.

FLYNN: Say, I'm runnin' this!

ROXIE: And I'm *payin'* for it!

FLYNN: And in advance—remember *that!* So don't get

cute or I'll throw the whole damn thing over—walk
out on you——

ROXIE [*throws chair to one side and starts after him*]:
You God-damned old crook!

FLYNN: Shut up, you dirty little——

> [*The door opens to admit* SUNSHINE *and* JAKE
> *and the* BAILIFF.]

JAKE: His Honor's here, Billy. [*To* ROXIE.] Come on,
Cinderella, the stage is set.

> [*There's an instant transformation.* FLYNN
> *gathers up his brief-case and hands* ROXIE *a bunch
> of lilies of the valley from the table, and she ad-
> justs her expression to wistful innocence, as she
> goes slowly to the door.*]

FLYNN [*in admiration and solemn tribute*]: A brave little woman!

> [*He follows immediately after her, then the*
> BAILIFF, *then* SUNSHINE *and* JAKE, *making a
> regular procession as* CURTAIN FALLS *and lights
> dim out to denote the passage of an hour or so.*]

SCENE 2

Afternoon same day.

*Judge Canton's Court, Criminal Court Building, Chi-
cago.*

*The "bench" with its high pulpit-stand is at the center
[rear]; the witness-box and jury seats at the left;
the clerk's desk, with phone and records, in the in-
closure at the right. There is a long table, left of
center, with chairs for the accused and bailiff, counsel*

*for the defense, attorney and runner for the State.
A high rail, with center passageway, shuts off the
common herd of listeners and furnishes a comfort-
able back for the pews of the privileged few: the
semi-circle at the right for relatives of the exhibiting
attorneys, visiting lawyers, politicians,—and O yes,
relatives of the deceased; that on the left, with its
narrow slanting table, for the representatives of the
press.*

*Windows on the right look out toward Clark Street; a
door at the left [extreme front] .leads to the jury
room and "bull-pen" for the accused; another [rear,
extreme right] to the Judge's chamber.*

Court is in session: his HONOR, *a closely shaven gentle-
man in the interesting forties, is on the Bench, and
his* BAILIFF, *a grizzled old chap, stands, gavel in
hand, just inside the rail of the inner sanctum, where
the* CLERK *hugs the Bible, well-worn—on the outside, at least. The* JURY, *a dozen of assorted sizes
with a preponderance of the middle-aged fatherly
type, are in the box; the* COURT REPORTER, *a near-
sighted dormouse, scribbles on and on.* MR. HAR-
RISON, *resplendent in a new suit;* MR. FLYNN, *com-
fortable in an old one; the accused and a sleepy*
BAILIFF—*all around the table.*

*A half dozen reporters in press seats; cameramen in the
sanctum at his* HONOR's *right, so they can have full
shot at jury, witness, and accused. Cameramen just
back of his* HONOR *for full shot at the auditors, counsel, and accused. Cameramen just inside the outer rail
for a close-up of witness and questioning attorney.
And then, just beyond the rail—in the wide passageway between general auditors and court proper—
movie men from a news weekly; real movie cameras*

*that grind and grind, and Klieg lights with their
eerie glare.*
*At present, however, they are not in action, and the
court is slightly relaxed.* Amos *is on the stand, and
the* Assistant State's Attorney *is reading to him
from a long typewritten paper. There's a fatuous
smile on his face, his eyes wander over the audience,
and he speaks slowly, eager to prolong the occasion.*
Mr. Flynn, *whose chair faces* Jury *and* Press *but is
carefully out of the* Judge's *vision, is working hard.
He listens with care to each word of his worthy op-
ponent, ready to register broadly the proper emotion:
amazement at his audacity, anger—anger barely restrained from physical violence—at the knavery of
the fellow, disgust at his chicanery, amusement at his
stupidity; and through them all a jolly camaraderie
with the* Jury—*a knowing look, a shake of the head,
a smile—they're not to be taken in, he knows that!
Ready also to spring up in objection.*
The Judge *and* Jury *may be listening to* Mr. Harrison—*they certainly hear his thundering tones—but
they rest their eyes—maybe feast their eyes—on a
fairer object than a dapper* State's Attorney *or the
gangling young man in green. You have guessed it,
gentle reader:* Roxie. *And who can blame them? For
the courtroom is hot and crowded and she wears that
dress with meaning. Her hair, soft and shining, is an
aureole in the sunlight. Her cheeks are a petal pink,
her parted lips a rose. She's working hard, too—
tilted forward on the edge of her chair, white hands
clasped to her breast.*

Harrison [*reads from typewritten paper*]: "Question
by Sergeant Murdock: 'What happened next?'

Answer by Roxie Hart: 'He—' [Casely] 'started for his hat and coat but didn't get that far.' Question by Sergeant Murdock: 'Why not?' Answer by Roxie Hart: [*Rings out brutally.*] 'Because, by God, I shot him!'"

[*There is a startled silence and* HARRISON *pauses. The* JURY *sits up sharply and looks shocked.* ROXIE *is astounded and turns to* FLYNN, *who half-rises in involuntary anger, then sinks back and pats her arm comfortably. Perfect teamwork.* HARRISON *reads:*]

"Signed, April the third: Roxie Hart." [*Hands paper to* AMOS.] Do you recognize the signature?

AMOS [*studies it carefully*]: I guess so. [*Beams at crowd.*]

HARRISON: Tell the jury.

AMOS [*leans back and tweaks suspenders*]: The lady who *used* to be My Wife.

HARRISON: Exactly! And weren't you at the police station when your wife—[*smiles pleasantly*] your *ex*-wife—made this confession?

AMOS [*drawls*]: Well, now, I don't know as I'd want to go so far as to say——

HARRISON [*paces nervously*]: Yes or no. . . . Didn't you hear her say those very words in answer to Sergeant Murdock's questions?

AMOS: *Some* of them—yes. . . .

HARRISON [*flings paper down in exasperation*]: What's your purpose in testifying? What are you——

FLYNN [*springs up*]: Your Honor, I object! The State's trying to discredit its own witness!

HARRISON [*hurls at* AMOS]: Why did you come to me and——

FLYNN [*excitedly*]: Your Honor, the sole purpose of

this questioning is to cast reflection upon the witness!

JUDGE [*in a bored tone*]: Sustained.

HARRISON [*stands a moment nonplussed, then turns on his heel in disgust*]: Take the witness.

FLYNN [*nods pleasantly to* AMOS]: You are at present divorced from the defendant?

AMOS: Yes, sir.

FLYNN: Who obtained this divorce?

AMOS: *I* did.

FLYNN: When did you file suit?

AMOS: May the fourth.

FLYNN: Was there any particular reason, Mr. Hart, for your filing suit on this exact day?

AMOS: Well, sir, the papers came out the day before with the story of—[*flounders*] the statement that she was—that there was goin' to be a little stranger . . .

FLYNN [*smiles broadly*]: Now, Mr. Hart, is that grounds for divorce!

AMOS [*wisely*]: Little too *much* of a stranger! [*Likewise gets a smile.*]

FLYNN: You mean by that you doubted the paternity of your child? [*Smiles again.*] I mean *the* child.

AMOS: Yes, sir. [*Warms up.*] And you can see how that made *me* look—like I was *easy.*

FLYNN [*smiling*]: And they can't put anything over on *you,* can they?

AMOS: *I'll* say they can't!

FLYNN: Had your wife apprised you of her condition prior to said announcement?

AMOS: How's that?

FLYNN: Had your wife told you about this "stranger"?

AMOS [*promptly*]: No, sir—neither one of 'em.

HARRISON: If counsel is going to pursue this line of inquiry further, your Honor, don't you think it would be advisable to exclude women from the room?

[REPORTERS *sit up animatedly and take down every word.*]

JUDGE [*with slow smile*]: If any lady wishes to leave, she may do so now. [ROXIE *starts up with alacrity and he adds, with another smile:*] Except the defendant.

FLYNN [*looks around at the crowd and calls out genially*]: That's right: stick to me, girls! [*To* AMOS.] Did you question her after you read it—talk it over with her?

AMOS: No-o——

FLYNN [*suddenly flames*]: Just took the word of a reporter—believed a vile story you read in some yellow paper——

HARRISON: Your Honor, I object: irrelevant and immaterial. Paternity and divorce have nothing to do with the murder of Fred Casely by Roxie Hart.

FLYNN [*wheels toward him*]: Paternity and divorce were introduced by you to besmirch the name of that defenseless girl! [ROXIE *drops her head modestly.*] Your Honor, I'm merely cross-examining on direct.

JUDGE [*very bored*]: Proceed.

FLYNN [*in lighter tone*]: Now, Mr. Hart, do you expect the jury to believe that—with all due respect to the press—[*Wave and bow toward them*—JAKE *gives a grin and salute in response*] our courts would grant you a divorce merely on a newspaper story?

AMOS: No, sir, I had a statement, that she'd made and signed herself, all about how she and this——

FLYNN: And where did you get this "statement"?

AMOS [*looks blandly toward* HARRISON *who frowns*]:
From the State's Attorney's office.

FLYNN [*nods comprehendingly*]: Oh—so the State's
Attorney's office gave you a statement that enabled
you to get a divorce, did it . . . that enabled you
to cast aside the woman you had sworn to love and
cherish—for better or worse. . . . [ROXIE *wipes
her eyes carefully.*] And *what*, Mr. Hart, did *you*
give the State's Attorney?

HARRISON [*springs up, hotly*]: Your Honor, this is too
much! [*To* FLYNN]. *Withdraw* that, *withdraw* that,
you——!

JUDGE: Gentlemen, gentlemen. . . . [*With reproach-
ful glance toward* FLYNN.] Counsel should be more
discreet.

FLYNN: All right, your Honor, I withdraw the question [*pause*] as unnecessary. [*To* AMOS.] You obtained your divorce then because you doubted the
legitimacy of this offspring?

AMOS: Yes, sir. I'm nobody's fool, I'm not.

FLYNN: And if you became convinced you were wrong
—had been hasty, you'd be man enough to admit it,
wouldn't you?

AMOS: Yes, sir.

FLYNN: You'd be willing, in fact, to take her back?

AMOS [*his eyes meet* ROXIE'S]: Yes, I'd take her back—
provided, of course——

FLYNN: Excused! [*Halts* AMOS *as he starts to leave.*]
One word more—just answer where you are: Can
you swear you are *not* the father of this child?

AMOS: We-ell—*no*—not exactly. . . .

FLYNN: Come here. [*They go to* JUDGE; REPORTERS
spring up and cluster about bench; hushed

conference while AMOS *shakes his head first* "*Yes,*" *then* "*No,*" *then* "*Yes,*" *to* JUDGE'*s questions.*] *That's*—all!

AMOS [*swings off*]: I ain't as dumb as I look.

HARRISON [*curtly*]: The State rests.

[*The* CLERK *calls in loud voice:* "*Roxie Hart!*" *A* MOVIE MAN *converses with the* JUDGE *hurriedly while cameras are adjusted. She takes the stand. Klieg lights flood the room with uncanny glares; the* JUDGE *straightens and looks judicial; the* LAWYERS *turn careful profiles to the camera, and the* JURY—*for this moment*—*look their sacred responsibility.*]

CLERK [*holds up Bible*]: Blahblahblahblahblahblahblah . . . truth . . . truth . . . truth . . . selp-yuh God.

ROXIE [*so bravely for all her fright*]: I do.
[*She is excited, she is thrilled: the crowds, the lights, the noise*—*all for her! She takes to it like a duck to water.*]

FLYNN [*takes his stand at her right*—*he doesn't want to cheat the camera: they must have at least a profile, preferably three-quarters*]: What is your name? [*He is looking at the* JURY, *but it is intent on the camera and does not answer.*]

ROXIE [*lifts eyes heavenward*]: Roxie Hart.

FLYNN [*flings his arm out with a magnificence that is alarming*—*the camera can't hear words*]: Where do you live, Mrs. Hart?

ROXIE [*closes her eyes with vampire passion and clasps one hand to her heart*]: Cook County Jail.

FLYNN [*a terrific impact of fist in palm and the famous Billy Flynn scowl*]: How old are you?

ROXIE: Twenty-three. [*Chokes the "three" so lip read-*

ers will not see, and wipes a tear from her eyes.]
     [*The camera has all it wants for a while; lights
     are gone, the grinding stops and there's general re-
     laxation from the terrific strain.*]
FLYNN: Let's see—where were we? O yes: were you
     acquainted with Fred M. Casely, the deceased?
ROXIE: Yes, sir.
     [*Note: From now on she's very much the plain,
     simple, honest and God-fearing working-girl.*]
FLYNN: When did you first meet him?
ROXIE: Ten minutes after five, September the eighth.
     [*Like all good witnesses she has mastered the mne-
     monic system recommended by Mr. A. of Seattle.*]
FLYNN: Where did this meeting transpire?
ROXIE: In the vestibule of the Waverly Company, 1861
     South Michigan Boulevard, Chicago, Illinois.
FLYNN: Relate to the jury what conversation, if any,
     took place between you on this date.
ROXIE: It was rainin' and I was standin' there with my
     girl friend lookin' out, for we didn't have any um-
     brella. And Mr. Casely came by and said, "It's a fine
     day for ducks," and we both said yes.
FLYNN: Both of you?
ROXIE [*after conscientious thought*]: Yes, sir, both of
     us. And he said he had an umbrella and would we
     care to walk to the car——
FLYNN: Car?
ROXIE: Street-car. And we said yes—[*forestalling his
     question*] she said yes, and we started out and be-
     fore we got to the corner he said his auto was there
     and he'd take us home. Well . . . you know how
     crowded a Cottage Grove car is at five-thirty on a
     rainy day when it gets to Eighteenth Street, and we
     said yes. And he did—her first, then me.

FLYNN: How did Mr. Casely conduct himself during this drive? [ROXIE *looks puzzled.*] Unusually—friendly in any way?

ROXIE: No, sir.

FLYNN: When was the next time you saw him?

ROXIE: The following Tuesday—it rained again and he took us home.

FLYNN: Both of you?

ROXIE: Yes, sir, both of us.

FLYNN: And the next time?

ROXIE: Thursday.

FLYNN: And then?

ROXIE: Friday. [*Apologetically.*] We had a kinda wet spell along then, you remember.

FLYNN: And was your friend with you each time?

ROXIE: O yes, sir.

FLYNN: Did you ever see Mr. Casely on any other occasions?

ROXIE: Yes, sir.

FLYNN: Where?

ROXIE [*innocently*]: Why, at the office.

FLYNN [*impatient at her dullness*]: Socially, I mean. Did he ever take you places?

ROXIE [*falters slightly*]: Yes, sir.

FLYNN: Do you recall the first place you went with him?

ROXIE: Yes, sir: the Policemen's Benefit Ball. [*She looks reproachfully at* OFFICERS MURDOCK *and* PATTERSON, *who are trying to hang her; they twist, uncomfortable.*]

FLYNN: When was that?

ROXIE: Christmas Eve.

FLYNN: Relate to the jury what conversation, if any, you had in regard to this ball.

Roxie: Well, one evening——
Harrison: I object, your Honor; time and place.
Flynn: Can you fix the time and place?
Roxie [*promptly*]: Five eighteen Tuesday, October
   the seventh, going south on Michigan Boulevard. And
   he said he had a couple of tickets to the ball, which
   was to be at the Coliseum and a very swell affair and
   he had been aimin' to take his sister and she couldn't
   go and would I care to and if I did and had nobody
   to go with, why *he'd* take me.
Flynn [*leans forward*]: Did you know at this time,
   Mrs. Hart, that he was *married?*
Roxie [*shocked*]: O *no*, sir! O *no*, Mr. Flynn!
Flynn [*with sad reproach*]: But *you* were married,
   Roxie.
Roxie [*drops her head*]: Yes, sir.
Flynn: You believe in the sacredness of the marriage
   tie, don't you?
Harrison: Your Honor, I object: what the witness be-
   lieves is immaterial.
Flynn: You know the marriage tie is sacred, don't you?
Roxie [*reverently*]: Yes, sir. . . . That's what I told
   him all along. . . .
Flynn [*in feigned surprise*]: Oh—so he had asked you
   before?
Roxie: O yes, sir—from the very start!
Flynn: Will you tell us, then, just why you made an
   exception for the Policeman's Ball?
Roxie [*in low tone*]: *I* dunno . . . so many things
   happen—and you don't know why. . . . [*Looks
   far-away and gives a long sigh.*] But I wouldn't
   have, I'm sure I wouldn't have, if my—if Amos—
   [*lips tremble and delicate pause*] Mr. Hart—and
   me hadn't quarrelled that mornin'.

FLYNN [*again surprised*]: Oh, did you and your—Mr.
Hart—quarrel?

ROXIE [*drops her head—life crushed within her, hope
beaten out*]: Yes, sir.

FLYNN: And who was to blame?

ROXIE [*flat, weary tone*]: *I* was, I guess . . . seems
like I couldn't stop pesterin' him. . . .

FLYNN: "Pestering him"—what about?

ROXIE [*flings her head back and a rich tone breaks
through*]: Because I wanted a *home!* I didn't want to
work—he was makin' his forty a week and I wanted a
. . real home—with children. . . . [*Her head droops
again. The* JURY *wipes its eyes.*]

FLYNN [*decides to forgive her and his tone is gentle*]:
I see. So conditions in your home caused you to——

HARRISON: Your Honor, I object to Counsel's drawing
conclusions as to——

FLYNN [*blandly*]: Strike it out. And so you drifted on
and on in this relation, unhappy——

ROXIE: O *most* unhappy!

FLYNN: *Why* were you unhappy?

ROXIE: Because I was deceiving my husband, and because I—[*fainter*] was doing . . . wrong. . . .

FLYNN: Why didn't you stop?

ROXIE: I *did* want to—I *tried* to—but he'd plead—Mr.
Casely—and say he couldn't live without me. . . .

FLYNN [*to* COURT REPORTER]: State's Exhibit D.
[*Hands paper to* ROXIE *and pauses a moment; then
his tone is cold: the subject is distasteful to him and
he has disgust for a man who would drag such matters
into a courtroom.*] In this you admit illicit relations with the deceased. [*She is in an agony of
shame.*] Is this statement true or false?

ROXIE [*in low tone*]: It's—true. [*She will not lie—you can feel that!—she will not lie!*]

FLYNN: You have heard other statements read to the jury, alleged to be made by you to Officer Murdock —I hand you State's Exhibits E and F. Are these true or false?

ROXIE [*energetically*]: False!

FLYNN: Do you accuse the State of changing——

HARRISON: Now, your Honor——

JUDGE: Rephrase your question.

FLYNN: Describe your state of mind at the time of the confession.

ROXIE: O I was all upset—frightened—worried— cryin'—laughin'——

FLYNN: Do you think it might be called hysterical?

ROXIE: Yes, sir, that's it: hysterical.

FLYNN [*pauses a moment, then speaks in deep, solemn tone*]: Roxie Hart, the State charges you with the murder of Fred Casely . . . guilty or not guilty?

ROXIE [*speaks first to* JUDGE—*then to* JURY]: Not guilty—O not guilty! I—I *killed* him, yes—but not —not the *other!*

FLYNN [*quietly*]: Do you remember Friday, April the third?

ROXIE [*low, steady tone*]: I do.

FLYNN: Tell the jury now, in your own way, the happenings of that day from five o'clock on. Take your time and speak clearly.

ROXIE [*turns to face the* JURY *directly—they perk up with interest*]: I left work as usual at five, took the Cottage Grove car, stopped at the A. & P. for some baking-powder for biscuits for breakfast next morning. . . . He was always so *fond* of my biscuits. . . .

FLYNN: Yes, yes. . . . [*Sympathetically.*] And what time was this?

ROXIE: About twenty uh six. . . . And I was just getting into a housedress when the doorbell rang. I thought it was Irma—my girl friend, and so I slipped on a sorto' kimona and went to the door.

FLYNN: Yes, and who was there?

ROXIE: It was Mr. Casely.

FLYNN: Who spoke first?

ROXIE: He did.

FLYNN: Do you remember what he said?

ROXIE: Yes, sir: "Hello, Roxie, I had to see you just once more!"

FLYNN: What did he mean by that?

ROXIE: I had written him a note telling him it was all over, that we must quit, for it could never end in happiness.

FLYNN: What brought you to this decision?

ROXIE: I had learned he was married, and . . . I realized I loved my husband . . . and perhaps we could be happy. . . .

FLYNN: And did he go away as you asked him to?

HARRISON [*shouting*]: I object to Counsel's feeding the witness!

FLYNN: I beg your pardon. . . . And what did *you* say?

ROXIE: I begged him to go away and tried to close the door, but he forced his way in! Then I told him to wait in the living-room while I dressed. . . . [*It's hard for her to go on*] . . . but he followed me into the bedroom. . . .

FLYNN: Yes? And then? [*Asks each question with an air of triumph.*]

ROXIE: I begged him to go, told him the neighbors would see him, that my husband would soon be home. . . .

FLYNN: And what did *he* say?

ROXIE: He'd been drinking and wouldn't listen. Finally he said if I'd take just *one* drink with him, he'd go. And I did.

FLYNN: What was the liquor? What kind was it?

ROXIE [*ingenuously*]: I don't know. It was in a bottle and tasted very bad.

FLYNN [*smiles*]: Bad liquor, or just tasted bad to *you*?

ROXIE [*seriously*]: Yes, sir.

FLYNN [*nods triumphantly*]: Why didn't you scream?

ROXIE: I was ashamed for the neighbors to know . . . you know how you'd feel. . . . [*Her eyes meet the butcher's and he nods.*] . . . And I'd kept tellin' him what I'd said in the letter—that no good would come of it, that I loved my husband——

FLYNN: Oh—you *told* him that you loved your husband? And what did he say to that?

ROXIE: It made him mad, and he said it didn't matter: I was his. And he kept trying to take me in his arms . . . [*Looks appealingly at* FLYNN *and hesitates.*]

FLYNN: Yes, Roxie: you must tell the jury *everything*. [*The* REPORTERS *sit up alert.*] They have a right to know. [*The* JURY *looks as if it's not only a duty but a pleasure.*]

ROXIE [*faint*]: And finally . . . I told him . . . my delicate condition. . . . [*The moment for which they have waited.*]

FLYNN: And what did he say to *that*?

ROXIE: He *swore*—[*looks shocked*] and said that he'd *kill* me before he'd see another man's child . . . [*The* REPORTERS *lick it up.*]

FLYNN: Where were you at this time?

ROXIE: By the victrola.

FLYNN: Show the jury. [*She scrambles to the diagram hanging on the wall.*] And Casely?

ROXIE: Here. [*Indicates bed.*]

FLYNN [*impressively as he hands her back to the witness chair with all the tenderness due a mother-to-be*]: Now, Roxie, tell the jury *just* what happened next.

ROXIE: The pillows were thrown back, and Mr. Hart's revolver was layin' there. He grabbed—I knocked it from his hand. It fell to the floor and he whirled me aside—back by the dresser now—and we both grabbed for the gun. I reached it first, then he started toward me. . . . I can see him now with that awful look in his eyes——

FLYNN: What kind of look? Describe it to the jury.

ROXIE: I can't describe it; but a terrible look—angry—wild——

FLYNN [*purrs*]: Were you afraid? Did you think he meant to kill you?

ROXIE [*shudders*]: O yes, sir! I knew if he once reached the gun. . . .

FLYNN [*purrs more deeply*]: It was his life then or yours?

ROXIE: Yes, sir. [*Faintly, as she lifts her eyes.*] And *not* . . . *just* mine . . . [*pause, then continues dramatic narrative*] . . . coming right toward me, with that awful look—that wild look . . . I closed my eyes . . . and . . . [*barely whispers*] . . . shot. . . .

FLYNN: In defense of your life?

ROXIE [*lifts her head nobly*]: . . . to save my husband's innocent unborn child!
FLYNN [*with wave of hand to* HARRISON]: Take the witness.

[*Black for an instant to denote the passage of several hours. It is late that afternoon and* FLYNN *is making his closing plea. He stands before the* JURY—*this is the hour he earns the five thousand. And Billy Sunday himself never worked harder, with muscle as well as brain, minus coat and collar, with perspiration standing in great beads on his forehead. He's fighting, gentlemen, fighting, with every drop of his blood, for the life of that brave little woman. The* JURY, *hypnotized, enthralled, hangs on each word and follows every gesture. The* PRESS *watch benignly; they know his whole bag of tricks, but* BILLY'S *always worth watching. Even the* JUDGE *listens.*

And ROXIE—? *This scene is really the close of an hour's duel between* ROXIE *and* FLYNN. *When the curtain goes up, honors are even and she is faithfully registering the emotions outlined for her in rehearsal. Gradually, however, she extends her field; deeper emotion, gesture, writhing. She works for her audience—the* JURY; *and they, fascinated, are torn between her contortions and the fervid orator.* FLYNN, *who feels them slipping, turns—when his speech permits—and tries to stop her with furtive gesture. Of course she is oblivious, and he is forced to redouble his own efforts— louder tone, wilder manner—to drown her out. Until toward the end you have them both playing in grand crescendo. . . .*]

FLYNN [*in low dramatic tone*]: Can't you see her that night? Alone! Alone! With only God and that—body. . . . [*Pause.*] You and I have never killed, gentlemen; *we* do not know the agony of that hour; we can only guess the mad regret, the bitter reproach, the torture, the *hell* [*he grinds it out like a minister*] she lived through then. The soul's Gethsemane. Alone. [ROXIE *droops in the approved manner—the* JURY *gives her a glance of sympathy, then is back with* FLYNN.] And into this sacred room rush the police. [*He snarls an imitation of* MURDOCK *and grasps an imaginary arm—*ROXIE *studies her wrist.*] "Why did you kill him? Come on now, yuh'd better *tell!*" Threats. Physical violence. . . . And the worthy State's Attorney! [*Sarcasm.*] With his kindness, his promises: [*Imitates* HARRISON *with a husky whisper*] "Come clean and I'll help you! Come clean and I'll get you off!" [ROXIE *follows, nodding eagerly, with a look of reproach at* HARRISON.] Frightened, hysterical, the girl breaks down. She *does* confess. Dazed and bewildered she says "yes" to whatever they ask her. . . . [*Takes statement from* COURT STENOGRAPHER.] Do *you* believe, gentlemen, that's a word-for-word confession he read you? Of *course* not! No human being could have made such a deliberate, coherent statement—certainly not this delicate, frightened girl. . . . No, there was careful selection; a bit here [*lifts out morsels from the air*]—a bit there—an addition, deletions—*anything* to build up his case! [*He's hoarsely confidential.*] He's *got* to bring home a conviction or LOSE HIS JOB! [*All eyes are turned in scorn toward* HARRISON, *who slinks down with eyes downcast.*] And then he read it to you: malicious

twist of meaning. . . . [*Reads as* HARRISON *read
in former scene:*]
. . . "but he didn't get that far. . . ."
"Question: 'Why not?' "
"Answer: 'Because, by God, I shot him.' "
That's the way he read it to you, ain't it!
   [JURY *looks grieved—it's true; he flings the
   paper on table.*]
He would have you believe, gentlemen, that child
sitting there [ROXIE *lifts her head—the picture of
girlish innocence*] SWORE. [*He is shocked—as the*
JURY *was that morning.*] Those were her words, yes,
but Ah! what a different meaning! This beast, this
drunken brute, who had forced his way into her
home—and remember, gentlemen, if she had shot
him down then, the law would have upheld her!—
was coming toward her, threatening her life. . . .
[*Breaks off and resumes in melancholy tone.*] What
was the future to her? Crushed, betrayed, broken-
hearted. . . . Nothing—*less* than nothing. But the
little life that fluttered beneath her heart—[*taps
his fountain-pen pocket*]—ah! mother-love stirred
within her . . . and those words were a tribute to
her Omnipotent Maker who stood by in her hour of
need: [*He brings it out with ministerial reverence—*
ROXIE's *gaze is directed heavenward and her hands
clasped to her heart in prayer.*] "By GOD I shot him."
   [JURY *looks relieved—effective pause while
   little Eva does her stuff. He goes on quietly.*]
I'm sorry she loved as she did. I'm sorry this mon-
ster preyed upon her innocence—I wish he had never
entered that happy little home. If sorrow could
avail [*he warms up*] Fred Casely would be here
now, for she'd give her life and gladly to bring

the dead man back! [ROXIE *nods in ecstatic confirmation and begins enthusiastic pantomime.*] But we can't do that, gentlemen. [*Melancholy.*] You may take her life as the State asks, but it won't bring Casely back. [*Gives* ROXIE *a fixed look. She recalls her cue and starts moaning and sobbing.*] And for what purpose? To protect society? [*His voice rings out.*] Do *you* fear that weeping girl? [*Finger darts to the tailor.*] Do *you?* [*To the hard-boiled egg in the corner.*] Do *you?* [*They don't—he continues.*] For her reformation? She learned her lesson, gentlemen, in that dark hour alone. For punishment? My *God,* she's punished enough! No—none of these! But to satisfy the greedy ambition of the prosecution! PROSECUTION? *No,* PERsecution! You are asked for a life, gentlemen—[*he turns in exasperation at the loudness of* ROXIE's *wails, and gives her a signal for quiet, which she sublimely ignores; he raises his voice to a shriek in the effort to drown her*] by one who would climb to fame on dead bodies! [*Pause, filled with her sobs, almost howls.*] We can't give her happiness—[*the* JURY *is with her*] no, it is too late for that. Betrayed, crushed, we can only let her pick up the broken fragments of life, the tangled threads—[*she's supposed to quiver her lip, but instead she rises, staggers toward the* JURY *with outstretched hands.*]—we can give her another chance! [*She totters, gives a wild shriek, and falls in a dead faint by his side. Grand confusion, and she's carried out. He turns to* JUDGE.] We rest, your honor; you may give the case to the Jury.

    [*Black for an instant to denote the passage of three or four hours.*]

[*Courtroom, ten o'clock that night. Gloomy and dull, with doors closed, and the* PRESS *awaiting verdict.* AMOS *strides in passageway;* JAKE *stands at vestibule door—half ajar, disclosing* BAILIFF *with ear to keyhole of jury-room;* MEN *and* WOMEN REPORTERS *lounge in press seats. A poker game has just finished among* CAMERAMEN *at* CLERK'S *desk, and* BABE *is giving imitation of* FLYNN *for* PHOTOGRAPHERS *and the lawyer himself, who watches from* JUDGE'S *doorway.*]

BABE [*stretches forth hands and exaggerates* FLYNN'S *manner*]: . . . And then kerflop! The purtiest faint I ever saw—and my camera not even set! And they carried her out just like a stiff! Or hypnotized—yuh could a stuck pins in her.

FIRST PHOTOGRAPHER: God, what a pitcher that would uh made! And this dirty bum— [*Gives* FLYNN *a shove.*]

FLYNN: That was a real faint, boys, an honest-to-God——

SECOND PHOTOGRAPHER: Tell it to Sweeney! Right at the end uh your speech!

FLYNN: It ended my speech, all right!

THIRD PHOTOGRAPHER: And her in there—dancin' the Charleston! [*With sudden inspiration.*] Make her do it again *now*—we could get her pitcher——

BABE: Naw, all they want now's the verdict . . . Good Lord, I wish— [*Suddenly.*] *I've* got it!

[*They fall to discussion;* FLYNN *joins the* REPORTERS.]

JAKE [*returns from vestibule*]: Well, they're through with the Klan and Prohibition, so there ought to be one before long.

FLYNN: What is it now?

JAKE: Ten to two. The drummer says he knew a jane like her once, and the third guy from the end—just pure cussedness!

> [*Flash, bang! Flash, bang! Flash, bang! Everyone stares in amazement—there's nothing to take pictures of; the cameras are not set, just the flashlight rods.*]

Hey there, what's the big idea?

BABE: Smokin' 'em out. If *that* don't bring 'em, it's Gabriel's cue!

> [*The* JUDGE *appears at the door from his chambers, and from the prisoner's room* [*left*] ROXIE—*minus her dress—peeps out.*]

Listen, Judge, can't we get a few pitchers now?

FIRST PHOTOGRAPHER: It's gettin' *late*, and if you want this with your oatmeal . . .

BABE [*yells to* ROXIE]: Come on, Red, we're shootin' 'em now! [*To* JUDGE.] You and her and counsel. . . .

AMOS: And me here with the ring and license.

BABE: Now if we just had the jury—couldn't yuh call 'em out for a minute?

FIRST PHOTOGRAPHER: Sure! Then we'd be through!

JUDGE [*in alarm*]: NO! That would be grounds for reversal. . . . I'm sorry, but . . .

FIRST PHOTOGRAPHER: Aw right, one uh her in her lawyer's arms.

BAILIFF [*rushes in, loud whisper*]: They're comin'! They're comin'!

> [FLYNN *hurries to prisoner's room to get his fair charge.*]

BABE [*grins*]: I knew that'd bring 'em!

[*All scramble to appointed places. The* JURY *files in;* ROXIE, *in exquisite orchid evening gown, enters on* FLYNN'S *arm;* FOREMAN *gives* JUDGE *envelope. There is an expectant hush—after all you never know, you know!*]

JUDGE [*reads*]: "We, the jury, find the defendant not guilty."

[*Flash, bang! Flash, bang! A shriek from* ROXIE, *cheers, confusion, and general bedlam all around. She kisses the* JUDGE, *the* STENOGRAPHER, *anybody else within reach: the* JURY *climbs over the rail. Pressed by her public she mounts the counsel table, flings her arms out in a carefully set speech delivered in her best artificial manner, while the* CAMERAMEN *go on with their pictures and the Klieg lights take up their glare.*]

ROXIE: Dear friends, kind friends, who have stood by me in the dark hours of the past: His Honor—Mr. Flynn—Mr. Callahan—[JAKE, *by the outer door, gives a look of disgust*] Mary Sunshine—and all you guys on the jury: you've been so kind to me— so—so *encouragin'*—that I'm goin' to do somethin' for you——

[*Bang, bang, bang! Three pistol shots from the corridor outside, then a woman's shriek. All stand poised a moment in tense silence.*]

JAKE: What the hell!

SUNSHINE [*avidly*]: Another murder!

[*A police whistle outside. As one man the crowd flings around from* ROXIE *and breaks for the door.*]

ROXIE: Hey, you! Come back here! [*They go steadily on.*] Wait a minute, I want to tell you something!

[*No one even gives her a look—she bursts into old-time rage.*] You God-damn bums walkin' out on me when I want to make a speech! [*Climbs down angrily and starts after them.*] It's important—it's *news!*

FLYNN [*only he and* AMOS *are left now*]: Forget it: you're all washed up!

ROXIE [*hopping around like a hornet*]: I am not washed up! I'm goin' in vaudeville—I'm famous!

AMOS: What!

ROXIE: Sure: booked solid for ten weeks!

AMOS: But the wedding——

ROXIE: No wedding! It would ruin my career!

AMOS: But the ring—[*takes from pocket and shows her*] platinum and diamonds this time!

ROXIE [*grabs it*]: I'll keep it to remember you by!

AMOS: But the baby, Roxie, the baby!

ROXIE: Baby! My God, do I look like an amachure!

BABE [*dashes in to his camera all set for action*]: Another case for you, Billy! [*Over his shoulder.*] It won't take a minute now, Captain: just a little pitcher of the two slayers with you here between 'em.

    [*They enter: a* POLICE SERGEANT *and a weeping, defiant* GIRL, *followed by* CAMERAMEN *and* REPORTERS, *who cluster about like flies . . . mosquitoes . . . buzzards.*]

JAKE [*to* BILLY]: Another jane out for trigger-practice —bumped off the boy friend, also his wife: gee, ain't God good to the papers!

ROXIE [*in spasm of jealousy and envy*]: Two of 'em —O my God!

JAKE: Come on, Carrots: a picture of you with Machine-Gun Rosie. [ROXIE *slides into position as she sees the cameras are set.*] "The Jazz-Slayer

Meets the Cicero Kid!" Shake hands! [*Poses them.*]

ROSIE: No! [*Jerks her hand away and flings arm up to cover her face.*] I don't want in the papers!

JAKE [*jerks it down again*]: Come on, sister, yuh gotta play ball: this is Chicago!

    [*The lights go on, the cameras grind; flash, bang,* CURTAIN!]

Watkins's *Chicago Tribune* Articles

Watkins's *Chicago Tribune* Articles

MYSTERY VICTIM IS ROBERT LAW; HOLD DIVORCEE

Mrs. Belle Gaertner Is Questioned
March 12, 1924, p. 1

Mrs. Belle Brown Overbeck Gaertner, a handsome divorcée of numerous experiences with divorce publicity, was arrested at an early hour this morning after the police had found the dead body of Robert Law, an automobile salesman, in her automobile.

Law had been shot through the head. His body was found slumped down at the steering wheel of Mrs. Gaertner's Nash sedan, a short distance from the entrance to Mrs. Gaertner's home, 4809 Forrestville avenue. On the floor of the automobile was found an automatic pistol from which three shots had been fired, and a bottle of gin.

Police Hear Shots.

The discovery of the shooting was made by Policemen David Fitzgerald and Morris Quinn of the Fiftieth street station. They were walking in Forrestville avenue soon after 1 o'clock. They saw a woman enter a sedan in which a man was seated. The two policemen went on to the corner of 50th street to pull the police call box. While they were at the box they heard three shots.

Hurrying back to the automobile they found that the woman had left the car. Law was dead. Then ensued a delay while the police sent for reinforcements and summoned the coroner. Upon the arrival of a coroner's assistant Law's name and address was found.

Denies Knowing of Death.

From the license number of the automobile Mrs. Gaertner's name and address were found. The police went to her apartment at 4809 Forrestville avenue and found Mrs. Gaertner hysterically pacing the floor. She readily admitted she had been with Law, but steadfastly denied she knew anything of the manner of his death.

"We went driving, Mr. Law and I," she told the police. "We started early in the evening and went to a place at 55th street and Cottage Grove avenue. There we got a quart of gin. Then we went to the Bingham cafe and had some drinks and lunch.

Tells of Fear of Robbers.

"We left the café about midnight and drove for a while. Then we drove up Forrestville avenue right near where I live. We were sitting there talking. Mr. Law said something about holdup men and said he was afraid of them. I don't know what happened next. I remember that I saw blood on his face. I was frightened. He didn't say anything and I didn't hear any shots. I just got out of the car and ran away."

Mrs. Gaertner was closely questioned as to her reason for leaving the car and returning to it. She denied this. She also denied, when pressed on this point, that she had gone to her apartment for a pistol.

Later she kept up her denial of any knowledge of the shooting. She finally admitted the gun was hers, saying she always carried it, because of her fear of robbers. When pressed concerning the actual shooting, she answered all queries with:

"I don't know, I was drunk."

Mrs. Gaertner Questioned.

After identification of Law's body had been made it was sent to a morgue. Mrs. Gaertner was taken to the 50th street police station for questioning. The police said she was hardly in condition to be questioned at length.

Robert Law, the victim of the shooting, was an automobile salesman. He was employed by the Nash sales agency at 2000 Michigan avenue. He is said to have been a friend of Mrs. Gaertner for only a short time.

Friends who knew of their affair said they had been driving and attending various functions together very much of late.

Her Marital Career.

Mrs. Gaertner has been twice married. She was Belle Brown, a cabaret singer. A number of years ago she married a man of the name of Overbeck, from whom later she was divorced. In September, 1917, she married William Gaertner, a wealthy manufacturer of scientific instruments with a plant at 5345 Lake Park avenue. The marriage was a Crown Point affair, the outcome of a romance of the south park bridle paths.

Only five months after their wedding Gaertner sued for an annulment on the ground that their marriage had occurred less than a year after her divorce. Just as this second marriage knot was to be severed they were married again and once more took to the bridle paths of Jackson park.

Life One of Sleuths.

This union lasted for three years and Judge McDonald on May 7, 1920, granted a divorce. It developed in the divorce hearing that they both had hired so many detectives that their home was filled and life was just one sleuth after another.

Trailed by Dannenberg.

One incident in the separation was a visit by Mr. Gaertner, accompanied by W. C. Dannenberg and others, to a house at 5345 Prairie avenue, where he found her with a man who said he was Edward Lusk. By an agreement in the decree Mrs. Gaertner received $3,000 and a lot of household furniture. With that she set up an establishment in Forrestville avenue.

Mr. Gaertner said last night at his home, 5227 Kimbark avenue, that he knew Mrs. Gaertner's whereabouts and that he had seen her occasionally in the three years since their divorce. "What has happened to her now?" he inquired.

HOLD DIVORCEE AS SLAYER OF AUTO SALESMAN

Story by Law's Pal Basis of Charge.
March 13, 1924, p. 1

Belva Gaertner, twice a divorcée of page one notoriety, was placed in the county jail last night, charged by a coroner's jury with slaying Walter Law, young automobile salesman.[1]

Law's body was found in her car early yesterday morning. He had been shot to death with a steel jacketed bullet after a cabaret gin party.

One minute of testimony from a pal of Law's brought the turning point in the inquest. It seemingly cleared all doubt from the minds of the jurors. The witness was Paul E. Goodwin, a fellow auto salesman.

Says Law Feared Woman.

"Walter told me Monday that he planned to take out more life insurance because Mrs. Gaertner threatened to kill him," Goodwin said under oath. "Three weeks before he told me she locked him in her flat with her and threatened to stab him with a knife, unless he stayed there."

That story, supplemented by a sentence or two of explanation seemed to sweep from the minds of the jury retold details of the gin party, the visible grief of Law's young wife and child, the story Mrs. Gaertner had told the police that she was so drunk she remembered nothing between leaving the cabaret and suddenly hearing a great explosion as Law toppled against her, dead.

The state, represented by Stanley Klarkowski, assistant state's attorney, had planned to have the inquest continued, but as Goodwin walked from the stand the prosecutor announced:

"The state is willing to let this case go to the jury at once, without further delay."

Divorcée Kept from Stand.

"Does Mrs. Gaertner wish to take the stand," asked Deputy Coroner Kennedy.

"She does not, on advice of counsel," replied Tom Reilly, one of her three attorneys, hired by her former husband, William Gaertner. "Her statement to the police has been admitted in evidence. That is all she cares to say."

Twenty minutes later the jury came back and the foreman read the verdict: "We, the coroner's jury, find that Walter Law came to his death in the automobile of Mrs. Belva Gaertner from a bullet fired by Mrs. Belva Gaertner."

Then came the recommendation that she be held without bail.

Goodwin's brief moment on the stand switched the entire complexion of the investigation. It brought the first direct intimation that Mrs. Gaertner had planned to make a target of the 29 year old man—some five to ten years her junior—who made her acquaintance through an automobile sale and retained it through midnight gin escapades.

Simple Gingham Café Idyl.

Prior to Goodwin's testimony the two hours of the inquest had been taken up with details, circumstantial and corroborative, but assembled it was simply this:

Belva and Walter got drunk at the Gingham café. They drove home. The car was found in front of her house. Law's body hanging over the steering wheel, her gun on the floor. She was found in her apartment, her clothes covered with blood, maintaining she was "so drunk" she couldn't remember anything. But she had said that at the café Law had proposed that they flip a coin to see which should have the first shot at the other, but that she had talked him out of the idea. The questions that arose at the inquest were:

Did she murder Law?

Did she shoot him in self-defense?

Did she accidentally shoot him?

Did he kill himself?

Did a third person do the slaying?

Wanted Law for Her Own?

"The motive which the state believes lies behind the case is this," Mr. Klarkowski said. "Mrs. Gaertner had ensnared Law. He tried to break away, to stick to his wife and family. She killed him rather than lose him."

Back of Goodwin's testimony lie further details not yet brought before the public. They are an amplification of his story, made partly by himself in private statements to officials, partly by other friends of the dead man.

Law, these details say, had feared Mrs. Gaertner for some time. He had repeatedly tried to break away from her, but she refused to let him go.

Law was depicted as "a boy who couldn't refuse" when women and gin were suggested. As recently as twenty-four hours before his death he confided in friends that "some day" he'd die—and probably at the hands of the woman with whom he went on drinking sprees once or twice a week.

"I believe that when Law and Mrs. Gaertner returned from the café she tried to make him enter her apartment," Mr. Klarkowski said. "He, remembering the time she locked him in and held him there at the point of a knife, refused. Then she pulled the gun, perhaps. He tried to stop her, but couldn't."

Prior to Goodwin's testimony there had been a succession of witnesses whose stories told nothing to refute the statement of Mrs. Gaertner that "we got drunk and he got killed—I don't know how."

Then Detective Sergeant Corcoran, who arrested Mrs. Gaertner, testified,[2] him, because he was so nice. Said she was too drunk to remember leaving the café—didn't know a thing until there was a big noise and Law toppled over."

"Curley" Brown, manager of the Gingham, about whom Mrs. Gaertner said she and Law had some words because she danced with Brown, gave a touch which, some thought, was satire. "They didn't have any gin," he said. "Just ginger ale. We don't allow gin. They didn't display any gun in the café—though they may have talked about one—for I've always got my eyes peeled for guns. They were such a nice couple—I'm certainly shocked."

Then, as people yawned and wondered if there'd be anything "hot," a detective whispered in Klarkowski's ear.

"Bring him in quick," said the prosecutor. And ten minutes later Goodwin took the stand.

NO SWEETHEART WORTH KILLING—MRS. GAERTNER

Belva Hopes for Jury of "Liberal" Men.
March 14, 1924, p. 17

No sweetheart in the world is worth killing—especially when you've had a flock of them—and the world knows it. That is one of the musings of Mrs. Belva Gaertner in her county jail cell and it is why—so she says—a "broad minded" jury is all that is needed to free her of the charge of murdering Walter Law.

The latest alleged lady murderess of Cook county, in whose car young Law was found shot to death as a finale to three months of wild gin parties with Belva while his wife sat at home unsuspecting, isn't a bit worried over the case.

"There Are Plenty More."

"Why, it's silly to say I murdered Walter," she said during a lengthy discourse on love, gin, guns, sweeties, wives, and husbands. "I liked him and he loved me—but no woman can love a man enough to kill him. They aren't worth it, because there are always plenty more. Walter was just a kid—29 and I'm 38. Why should I have worried whether he loved me or whether he left me?"

Then the double divorcee of frequent newspaper notoriety turned to the question of juries.

"Now, that coroner's jury that held me for murder," she said. "That was bum. They were narrow minded old birds—bet they never heard a jazz band in their lives. Now, if I'm tried, I want worldly men, broad minded men, men who know what it is to get out a bit. Why, no one like that would convict me."

This Worries Her.

A long laugh and then a frown.

"But, I wish I could remember just what happened. We got drunk and he got killed with my gun in my car. But gin and guns—either one is bad enough, but together they get you in a dickens of a mess, don't they. Now, if I hadn't had a gun, or if Walter hadn't had the gin—" Of course, it's too bad for Walter's wife, but husbands always cause women trouble."

No attempt was made yesterday to get Mrs. Gaertner out on bail, and it is not likely one will be made before the grand jury acts. Prosecutor Stanley Klarkowski hopes to get the case before the jury tomorrow or Monday and is convinced there will be an indictment.

And, while Mrs. Gaertner chortled in jail, plans were completed for young Law's funeral today. It will be held from his home and will be private.

WOMAN PLAYS JAZZ AIR AS VICTIM DIES

April 4, 1924, p. 1

For more than two hours yesterday afternoon Mrs. Beulah Annan, a comely young wife, played a foxtrot record named "Hula Lou" in her little apartment at 817 East 46th street. Then she telephoned her husband and reported that she had killed a man who "tried to make love" to her.

The Hawaiian tune was the death song of Harry Kolstedt, 29 years old, of 808 East 49th street, whom Mrs. Annan shot because he had terminated their little wine party by announcing that he was through with her. His body lay hunched against the wall in her bedroom as she played the record over and over again.

When taken to the Hyde Park station by the police Mrs. Annan protested tearfully that she had killed Kolstedt to save her honor.

Made Himself at Home.

"He came into my apartment this afternoon," she said, "and made himself at home. Although I scarcely knew him, he tried to make me love him. I told him I would shoot. He kept coming anyway, and I—I did shoot him."

Soon after midnight, however, after the fumes of the liquor had worn away, she told a different story to Assistant State's Attorneys Bert A. Cronson and William F. McLaughlin. For hours they had questioned her without breaking down her story.

Then, with Capt. Edward Murnane of the Hyde Park station, they took the woman back to her apartment. There she was forced to stand in a dim light, facing the scene of the murder, while questions were fired at her in monotonous succession.

Breaks Down Under Quiz.

"What about the blood on the phonograph record? What about the wine and gin bottles and empty glasses? How come that Kolstedt was shot through the back?" Mrs. Annan was asked.

Finally she broke down.

"You are right; I haven't been telling the truth," the young woman admitted. "I'd been fooling around with Harry for two months. This morning, as soon as my husband left for work, Harry called me up. I told him I wouldn't be home, but he came over anyway.

"We sat in the flat for quite a time, drinking. Then I said in a joking way that I was going to quit him. He said he was through with me and began to put on his coat. When I saw that he meant what he said, my mind went in a whirl and I shot him. Then I started playing the record. I was nervous, you see."

As she played, Mrs. Annan began to wonder about her husband. What would he say when he came home and found a dead man lying in his bedroom? So at ten minutes before 5 she telephoned him at the garage at 9120 Baltimore avenue, where he is employed.

"I've shot a man, Albert," she told him. "He tried to make love to me."

Husband Hurries Home.

Annan hurried home in a taxicab and found his wife in a hysterical condition. Kolstedt, in his shirt sleeves, was hunched against the wall. Near by were his coat, hat, vest, and overcoat. Mrs. Annan's clothing was stained with blood.

Annan picked up the telephone to call the police. His wife threw herself on him, imploring him not to. At that instant the connection was completed, and the voice of Sergt. John O'Grady sounded over the wire from the Wabash avenue station. Mrs. Annan snatched the receiver.

"I've just killed my husband!" she shrieked. In reply to the sergeant's question she mumbled her address. The receiver clicked.

When detectives reached the apartment they found Mrs. Annan— a beautiful woman of 28, slim and tall, with reddish brown hair bobbed to the mode—waiting with a fanciful story of having fainted after shooting Kolstedt.

DEMAND NOOSE FOR 'PRETTIEST' WOMAN SLAYER

Mrs. Annan Held on Murder Charge.
April 5, 1924, p. 1

By Maurine Watkins.

Beulah May Annan, the 23 year old wife who shot "the other man" Thursday afternoon to the tune of her husband's phonograph,[3] was held to the grand jury yesterday afternoon by a coroner's jury, which charged her with the murder of Harry Kolstedt. Assistant State's Attorneys Bert Cronson, Roy Wood, and William McLaughlin are preparing to rush the case to an early trial, at which they will ask the death penalty.

Thursday afternoon Mrs. Annan played "Hula Lou" on the phonograph while the wooer she had shot during a drunken quarrel lay dying in her bedroom at 817 East 46th street. And yesterday afternoon the chapel organ at Boydston's undertaking parlors played "Nearer, My God to Thee" for an old soldier's funeral, while she waited for the inquest to start.

Changes Her Story.

Thursday night at the Hyde Park station she insisted that Kolstedt's advances had caused her to shoot to save her honor. Several hours later, however, when the effect of the liquor had worn off, she broke down hysterically and confessed that she had lied; that Kolstedt had threatened to leave her, and that she had killed him rather than lose him. But yesterday she only shook her head dreamily and smiled when questioned.

"I wish they'd let me see him," she said softly. "Still, it would only make me feel worse." The last time she saw him was when he lay dying and she dare not feel his heart or pulse because he was "so bloody."

They say she's the prettiest woman ever accused of murder in Chicago—young, slender, with bobbed auburn hair; wide set, appealing blue eyes; tip-tilted nose; translucent skin, faintly, very faintly, rouged, an ingenuous smile; refined features, intelligent expression— an "awfully nice girl" and more than usually pretty. She wore fawn colored dress and hose, with black shoes, dark brown coat, and brown georgette hat that turned back with a youthful flare.

Talks of Little Son.

While waiting for the inquest she talked of her early life in Kentucky and her little 7 year old son by a former marriage, who now lives with his father's people in Owensboro, Ky. Divorced from Perry Stephens after a year, she moved to Louisville, where she met Albert Annan, her present husband, whom she married in Chicago four years ago. He made $50 or $60 a week as mechanic at a garage at 9120 Baltimore avenue, but she wanted to work, too, and last September became bookkeeper for Tennant's Model laundry.

It was there she met Harry Kolstedt, another employee, who took her for walks, visited her a few times in her husband's absence, and shared with her a taste for "booze."

Repeats Her First Story.

Calmly she played with a piece of paper and softly whistled through it as Kolstedt's brother-in-law, William Wilcox, told the coroner's jury what she had told him of the tragedy the night before. He also identified the statement read by Assistant State's Attorney Roy Woods as the one she had made in his presence the preceding night.

According to this, Kolstedt had telephoned her early Thursday morning that he was going over on the west side to get some wine, and had come to her apartment fifteen minutes later to get the money with which to buy it. She had the afternoon off from work, and he joined her at about noon with two quarts of wine. After drinking for an hour or so they started quarrelling. She teased him a little about "Billy, the boy with an auto," and he reproved her for doing things she shouldn't. Then she flared back: "You're just a four-flusher!" and called him a "jail-bird." Kolstedt, it seems, had served a penitentiary sentence for a statutory crime. He retorted hotly that she was "no good."

A revolver was lying on the bed, and both sprang—

"Both went for the gun!" interrupted W. W. O'Brien, counsel for Mrs. Annan. "Both sprang for it."

But she reached it first, the story went on. Kolstedt turned for his coat and hat but "didn't get that far."

She cupped her chin in a slim white hand, with its orange blossom ring, and didn't blanch as the state read her answer to the question.

"Why didn't he get that far?"

"Darned good reason: I shot him."

She caught him as he slipped to the floor, calling, "My God! You've shot me!" and tried to tell him it wasn't true. His hands still felt soft, his face was soft, but she couldn't feel his heart for it was "all bloody."

She played again with the paper as the state's attorney read her confession of intimacy with Kolstedt on three occasions and laughed lightly as the lawyers quarreled over the questioning.

According to the testimony of Policeman Thomas E. Torton, who was called at 6:05 o'clock Thursday night, the shooting must have occurred at approximately 2 o'clock. For almost four hours, then, she played the phonograph and paced the floor before she telephoned her husband that she had killed a man. Upon his arrival they called the police and physicians. Dr. Clifford Oliver, who arrived at 6:20 o'clock, said Kolstedt had been dead only half an hour or so.

Husband on Stand.

Mrs. Annan had posed prettily for the photographers, but her husband hid his face with his rough, scarred hands when he took the stand. He identified the revolver—a .38 caliber—as his, and haltingly told how he had found the man—whom he did not know—dead and his wife too hysterical to talk.

Thursday night at the station he told the officers bitterly: "I've been a sucker, that's all! Simply a meal ticket! I've worked ten, twelve, fourteen hours a day and took home every cent of my money. We'd bought our furniture for the little apartment on time and it was all paid off but a hundred dollars. I thought she was happy. I didn't know—"

But yesterday he wouldn't talk; just shook his head sadly to all questions.

Under advice of her attorney, Mrs. Annan made no statement.

When the finding of murder was announced she powdered her nose, took the money her husband had borrowed, and went back to jail to await developments.

BEULAH ANNAN SOBS REGRET FOR LIFE SHE TOOK

Lives Through Crime Again as She Awaits Trial.
April 6, 1924, p. 4

By Maurine Watkins.

"Of course I'm sorry! I'd give my life to have Harry Kolstedt alive again! And I never said I was glad. Why, I couldn't. Why—" and tears filled the eyes of Mrs. Beulah May Annan, the "prettiest murderess," held to the grand jury for shooting her sweetheart in a drunken quarrel at her apartment on Thursday.

Thursday night, a mad, hysterical frenzy, when she babbled conflicting accounts of the murder. Friday, a daze that left her cold and unmoved at the inquest. But yesterday afternoon in the county jail, where she awaits indictment for murder, she began to realize what it means to kill.

And the music changed, too. "Hula Lou," on the phonograph while the lover she shot lay dying; a funeral song in the chapel, when she awaited the inquest, and yesterday "Bring them in from the fields of sin!" sung by prisoners indicted or sentenced for robbery, prostitution, and murder.

Inmates Jar on Her.

It jars on her horribly—the laughter of the girls, their constant talking, the music.

"How can they!" she said, shivering.

She posed for her picture with Mrs. Belva Gaertner, whose trial for the shooting of Law, the young auto salesman, begins on April 21, but as yet the two have not talked over their common interests.

A man, a woman, liquor, and a gun—

But unlike Mrs. Gaertner, who waits cheerfully and philosophically, protesting her innocence and disclaiming all recollection of the killing, Mrs. Annan remembers.

"Never Forget It."

"I'll never forget it." She shuddered. "That white silk shirt—all covered with blood! He never spoke or moved, just lay there—I know he died as soon as he fell. And I was with him—dead," here eyes widened in horror,[4] "for two or three hours. I never thought of a doctor until the policemen came, and when they said he might be alive—O, it was the happiest moment in my life!"

She remembers, too, just how it happened.

"I had learned that morning—just before I came home—that he had been in the penitentiary, and I accused him of it. And he grew angry and—but it wouldn't have happened if we both hadn't been drinking; and he had had quite a lot before he came over. We both lost our heads, saw the revolver lying there uncovered by the pillow, for I hadn't made the bed that morning, and grabbed for it. I can see him now—that look in his eyes! He was perfectly wild, and I know he would have killed me if I hadn't reached it first."

Disclaims Early Statements.

Her lawyer, W. W. O'Brien, stated Friday that self defense would be her plea and that the statements made at the police station would be repudiated as having been made under duress when intoxicated.

"I listened when they read the statement at the inquest, and—" she hesitated—"some of the things were right. But the newspapers are all wrong," she went on. "They say I killed him rather than have him leave me. Why, I was the one who was going to quit him. You see, I realized that we wouldn't go on, that we could never really be anything to each other. I never loved him as much as I did 'my hubby'—and, besides, he had nothing to offer me, no inducement to make me leave Albert. It had gone on as long as it should. I knew no good could come of it—" Her voice trailed off in a long sigh.

Husband Back at Work.

And Albert Annan, the man to whom[5] what did "come of it" was a total shock, for he never dreamed of her other love interest, is going ahead with his work in the garage and giving what money he can to help her out.

"What'll I do when it's over? I don't know. There's not much use to think about that. Albert probably won't want me back—my life's ruined anyway; I can never live it down. Even if I went away where nobody knew you can't get away from yourself. And I'd always remember that I'd killed him. Always see that white shirt and the blood!" and she broke into sobs.

Her attorney hopes to arrange bond for her in a couple of weeks and is hoping for a speedy trial.

MRS. ANNAN HAS LONESOME DAY BEHIND THE BARS

April 7, 1924, p. 14

Mrs. Beulah Annan's second day in the county jail, where she waits indictment for the murder of her sweetheart, Harry Kolstedt, was a trifle monotonous.

"Sunday's bad enough any place, but here—" and Chicago's prettiest woman "killer" shrugged her shoulders in disgust. She misses the conveniences of home—they won't even let you have cold cream and powder! And they tuned in the radio for a sacred concert instead of Hawaiian fox trots.

Thinks of Bonds.

And the uncertainty's growing tiresome. Will the grand jury indict her this week? Will she get bond? Will her father, John Sheriff, Kentucky farmer, furnish the money? For she hasn't heard from him since the arrest, nor from her mother, Mrs. Mary Neal, who moved from 4919 Lake Park avenue Saturday night and left no address because she didn't want to be "bothered."

But the husband, Albert Annan, who knew nothing of the "other man" till he found the dead body in his apartment, is "standing by." Yesterday afternoon he bundled up some clothes   a black crepe dress and a checkered flannel—and took them down to the jail. But Sunday isn't visiting day, so he went back "home" to the little flat at 817 East 46th street, where his wife had killed a man in a drunken quarrel. They'll have to sell the furniture now, bought last November and all paid for except $100.

Husband Still Faithful.

There an hour or so later he repeated his steady refusal: "Nothing to say," and set his jaw determinedly. Ten years older than Beulah May, he is quiet and a little stern. He had talked to her only once since the tragedy—at the Hyde Park station, when he tried to shoulder the blame by saying he'd killed Kolstedt when he found the two together.

"Tell her I'll stick—that's all—that I'll stick," he said slowly.

He's getting off from work today—he's a mechanic at a garage at 7190 Baltimore avenue—to see her attorney, W. W. O'Brien, about getting bonds.

"We've got to get her out," he said fiercely.

Others are helping to while away the hours for Beulah. A group of young men, admittedly after having a "few drinks," sent flowers with a note. And she didn't eat the chicken dinner he had planned for her; for a "friend" sent in a juicy steak, French fried potatoes, and cucumber salad.

WOMAN GIVEN LIFE IN JAIL AS MURDERESS

May 8, 1924, p. 1

Mrs. Elizabeth Unkafer, 46 years old, was given a life term in Joliet penitentiary by a jury that found her guilty last night of the murder of Sam Belchoff, a street car conductor, some months ago. The jury was out two hours and took three ballots.

As the words fixing her punishment were read in Judge Frederic DeYoung's court, the woman threw back her head, clinched her teeth and gazed at the ceiling. Her wrinkled face and faded red hair shown brightly under the lights above the judge's bench.

Disbelieve Insanity Plea.

The defense that she was insane both at the time of the killing and at present was met successfully by Assistant State's Attorneys Emmet Byrne and Rudolph Shapiro, according to the jurors after they were discharged. They stated further that they believed the constant mumbling and talking of the woman during the trial was an attempt at feigning insanity.

Attorneys for the defense asserted the woman's mind was subnormal due to a social disease. They produced a number of witnesses who testified that in their opinion she was insane. The prosecution brought forward the testimony of well known alienists who found her to be normal mentally.

Third to Be Sentenced.

Mrs. Unkafer is the third woman to receive a life term in Cook county up to date, the others being Mrs. Tillie Klimek, who poisoned three husbands, and Mrs. Katherine Baluk-Malm, who killed a watchman in a holdup. Katherine Malm was the first to greet Mrs. Unkafer upon her return to "murderesses' row" in the jail.

Belchoff was killed after he declared he was "through with her" while the couple was sitting in the woman's bedroom at 1458 West Madison street on February 3.

BEULAH ANNAN AWAITS STORK, MURDER TRIAL

Jail Women Wonder 'What Jurors Think About.'
May 9, 1924, p. 6

By Maurine Watkins.

What counts with a jury when a woman is on trial for murder? Youth? Beauty? And if to these she adds approaching motherhood—?

For pretty Mrs. Beulah Annan, who shot her lover, Harry Kohlstedt,[6] to the tune of her husband's phonograph, is expecting a visit from the stork early this fall. This 23 year old murderess, now waiting trial, is making this the basis for a further appeal to clemency.

Couldn't Take Two Lives.

Because of the "four-term" rule, Mrs. Annan's case cannot be continued for more than four terms of court without her consent. If she is brought to trial before autumn her condition can be considered by the jury, since it has the right to pass sentence. If the jury should give her death—

"There is no direct statute covering such contingency," said a former state's attorney, "but the state would have to delay execution till after the birth of the child, since it would be taking two lives instead of one."

"Her condition has no bearing upon the legality of the case," said her attorney, William Scott Stewart. "It would be a matter of executive clemency, once the sentence was passed. Or it might affect the jury."

What Influences a Jury?

Will a jury give death—will a jury send to prison—a mother-to-be?

What affects a jury anyway? That's what they asked themselves, the seven inmates of "Murderess' Row," yesterday afternoon, for the conviction of one of their number broke the monotony of their life and startled them into a worried analysis. And Elizabeth Unkafer, the "queer" one, who received "life" for the leap year murder of her lover, Sam Boltschoff, held the spotlight for a few brief hours.

"They gave her 'life' because she killed a man! I have killed a man: will they—" then they gamely shake their heads-no, it can't be life for them! "What counts most with a jury after all?"

Sex.

"A woman never swung in Illinois," said one triumphantly.

Looks. [Elizabeth Unkafer was not cursed with fatal beauty!]

Jurors Have Eyesight.

"A jury isn't blind," said another, "and a pretty woman's never been convicted in Cook county!" Gallant old Cook county!

Youth. (Elizabeth was 43.)[7]

Kitty Malm who received "life" for shooting a watchman last November, is said to be the only really young woman who's ever gone over the road, and Kitty wasn't—well—quite "refined."

Of the four awaiting trial, the cases of Mrs. Annan and Mrs. Belva Gaertner would seem most similar to Elizabeth Unkafer's; each is accused of shooting a man, not her husband, with whom her relations were at least questioned: each is supposed to be "a woman scorned" who shot the man "rather than lose him." But neither was at all disconcerted by Mrs. Unkafer's sentence.

"I can't see that it's anything at all like my case," said Mrs. Gaertner, the sophisticated divorcée indicted for shooting Law, the young auto salesman, as she twirled about in her red dancing slippers.

"The cases are entirely different," said Mrs. Annan, quite the ingenue in her girlish checked flannel frock.

Lizzie Was No Beauty.

No, Elizabeth, with her straggly mop of red hair, pale eyes, and flabby cheeks, remembers it all too well. She paused in her scrubbing the jail floors yesterday afternoon to live it all over again.

Her attorney had pleaded "insanity."

"Think I'm goin' to say I'm crazy?" she asked indignantly. "Not much! They'd lock me up then with some that are worse than I am—and no tellin' then what would happen! I wanted 'em to shoot me—why not?—at State and Madison—make a big day of it, and give every one a front seat, but they gave me life instead."

SELECT JURY TO PRONOUNCE FATE
OF BEULAH ANNAN
May 23, 1924, p. 6

By Maurine Watkins.

Beulah Annan, the pretty slayer on trial in Judge Lindsay's court for the murder of Harry Kalstedt, her lover, smiled and pouted, sighed and turned r.s.v.p. eyes on the jury, as the attorneys selected in just one day the twelve "good men and true" who will decide her fate. The jurors are:

David L. Williams, 3949 Grenshaw street; Patrick Mullen, 802 South California avenue; Harry A. Dunham, 18 South Dearborn street; Le Roy H. Dey, 5413 Race avenue; Harold J. Gorman, 1540 East 65th place; Walter F. Born, 512 North Laramie; John Manning, 4918 St. Anthony court; Leonard W. Jones, 3704 Maple square; James Dalzell, 6915 South Western; William G. Hodgson, 1427 Harding avenue; Fred Mutter, 1964 Farragut avenue.

And they're a good looking lot, comparatively young, and not too "hard boiled"—for Beulah herself passed on them. And she's a connoisseur in men! Perry Stephens, who divorced her down in old Kentucky; Al Annan, the husband who's "standing by"; Harry Kalstedt, the farmer boy she killed—

Acts the Czarina.

A nod of her pretty bobbed head: four bachelors were accepted as jurors. A pouting "no"; peremptory rejection by her attorney, William Scott Stewart.

A dozen or so were excused because they had "fixed opinions" as to the guilt of the girl who had confessed to the police that she shot young Kalstedt in the back April 3 in her husband's apartment of 46th street, when he told her he was "done" and started to leave after a quarrel.

"Too damned many women gettin' away with murder!" growled one man excused from jury service.

"I'd have given her the rope, I would!" said another as he was dismissed for "cause."

Only one man excused was for "acquittal."

"Kalstedt got what was coming to him—the fool! In a married woman's apartment!" he said.

Didn't Like Salome.

Prohibition struck off four or five more, who confessed they might be prejudiced against a modern Salome who killed a man after a drinking party—and then played jazz while he lay dying.

The state, represented by Roy C. Woods and William F. McLaughlin, dismissed those who said they weren't sure of the effect a pretty woman might have on them.

For she is admittedly the prettiest murderess Cook county has ever known and was an appealing figure yesterday in her simple fawn colored suit with dark brown fur piece that framed the flowerlike face— still pale from her recent illness. Only 23, slender, with wide blue eyes and a halo of auburn curls, freshly marceled—and "by the advice of counsel" she kept her head bare.

Early in the trial she leaned wearily on one white hand—with Raphaelite profile turned toward the jury—and pensively sighed now and then. But she revived sufficiently to powder her nose and pose for some pictures while she chatted of her recent illness.

W. W. O'Brien, associated with Mr. Stewart in the defense, stated that they would admit the crime, but plead self-defense, proving that Mrs. Annan and Kalstedt struggled for the revolver and that she shot him to save her own life.

The state did not qualify the jury for the death sentence, but they may ask it, as they expect to prove it was "a cold blooded, dastardly murder."

JUDGE ADMITS ALL OF BEULAH'S KILLING STORIES

Which of Them Will Jury Credit?
May 24, 1924, p. 1

By Maurine Watkins

"Beautiful" Beulah Annan's chance for freedom was lessened yesterday when Judge Lindsay ruled, after an extended hearing, that the confessions she had made to the police the night following the murder of Harry Kalstedt, April 3, were admissible as evidence.

"I'm the only witness," Beulah has boasted. "Harry's dead and they'll have to believe my story."

But which one?

The confession she made to Assistant State's Attorney Roy C.

Woods (with a court reporter present) in her apartment at 9 o'clock the night of the crime, when she said that she shot Kalstedt, whom she barely knew, to save her honor as he approached her in attack?

Second Story Different.

Or the statement that she made at the Hyde Park police station (also with court reporters present) three hours later? Then she broke down and admitted that she shot him in the back.

The man was about to leave her after a jealous quarrel, she said. Will the jury believe that?

Or will the jury credit the story that she'll tell in court, a plea of self-defense: "We both grabbed for the revolver!"—when she takes the stand today?

Pale, not quite so pretty, Beulah didn't smile as she took the stand yesterday morning to help her attorneys, Wm. Scott Stewart and W. W. O'Brien, prove that she had been unduly influenced and offered immunity by the state, if she would make a statement. Slim and straight in her new brown satin crepe frock, with furpiece thrown over one arm, she walked carelessly to the stand, moistened her lips, and was sworn in; seemingly calm, but her answers, keyed only for the judge, in the absence of the jury, were weak.

Shows Strain of Ordeal.

Q.—Who was the first person to arrive at your apartment after the shooting? A.—Officer Torpy.

Q.—What did he say? A.—"Where is the gun?"

Q.—What did you say? A.—My husband gave him the gun. And I don't remember much else.

Q.—Whom did you see next? A.—Assistant State's Attorney Woods.

Q.—Now you had fainted during the time that you saw Torpy and Mr. Woods? A.—Yes.

Q.—What did Mr. Woods say? A.—Well, we went into the kitchen and he said, "Don't you know me?" and I said "No." And he said, "I am

Roy C. Woods, and I am a customer of Mr. Wilcox and a personal friend of his." Then he told me not to be afraid, that I had shot the man in my own house, and that it was no crime.

This evidence was uncontradicted by the state since Mr. Woods, as prosecutor in the case, could not take the stand, but Judge Lindsay indicated in his talk with counsel that he gave it slight credence.

"Her statements are entirely too vague," he said crisply. "Moreover, it is peculiar that she was so intoxicated that she didn't know what had happened a few hours after the crime, and today has a perfect recollection of minute details."

W. W. Wilcox, brother-in-law of the dead man, testified that no one had tried to force Beulah to make the statements or had promised her immunity.

Wilcox Accuses Beulah.

"However, she tried to get it," he stated. "She asked Woods if he couldn't 'frame' it to look like an accident, and Woods said, "You don't 'frame' anything with me." He stated further that Beulah seemed perfectly natural the night of the crime, seeming a little sorry now and then, but smiling most of the time.

Albert Allen, the court reporter who had taken both of her confessions, testified that she had made them with full understanding that they might be used against her, and that they were voluntary and of her own free will. Police officers gave testimony to the same effect, though they admitted she was in a "high-sterical" condition for several hours.

Counsel for the defense objected in particular to the admissions of state's exhibit two (the midnight confession) as in it Mrs. Annan confessed to intimacy on various occasions with the man she afterwards killed.

"We're not trying a case of adultery, judge," objected W. W. O'Brien.

Judge Lindsay, however, ruled that admission was relevant to the case.

Like Wide Eyed Kitten.

Beulah, frankly bored by such technicalities, stared around the room like a wide eyed kitten and gave her attention only when Assistant State's Attorney William F. McLaughlin read the two confessions.

According to the first statement, Kalstedt had come to her house early in the afternoon—greatly to her surprise, for she barely knew him. He took off his coat and hat, then turned and tried to take her in his arms, saying, "with a look in his eyes," "Gee, Ann, I'm crazy about you."

She begged him to go, she said, but he refused, and followed her into the bedroom, where she reached for the revolver, which was lying under a pillow on the disarranged bed. Then she closed her eyes and shot as he approached her.

"But he was shot in the back," they told her.

Version State Approves.

It was this fact which caused her to make a new statement, giving what the state believes is a true account of the affair.

Beulah listened with set features to the reading of her admission that she had given Kalstedt, whom she had known for several months at Tennant's laundry, where she was employed as bookkeeper, a dollar to get some wine to bring to her apartment Thursday afternoon— her afternoon off. He came about half past twelve and they started the party.

Q.—How much did you drink? A.—Half a gallon.

Q.—The two of you? A.—Yes. We had an argument.

Q.—What about? A.—Well, I heard he had been in jail, and I asked him about it.

Q.—What did he say? A.—He said he had. And then I told him he had always told me he had a lot of money, and his people were sending him money.

Refused Another Date.

The questions then related to a certain "Billy," who had called Mrs. Annan that morning for a "date," which she had refused for Kalstedt.

Q.—Did he say anything to you about your having done things that you shouldn't? A.—O, yes, and I said to him: 'Well, you're nothing!'

Q.—Did you call him anything? A.—Yes.

Q.—What did he say then? A.—He jumped up.

Q.—Did he say anything to you about being through with you? A.— O, he may have said, "To hell with you" or something like that.

Q.—When was that? A.—After I had told him he was a jail bird and didn't have any money.

Q.—Then you say he jumped up? A.—I was ahead of him. I grabbed for the gun.

Q.—And what did he grab for? A.—For what was left—nothing.

Q.—Did he get his coat and hat? A.—No, he didn't get that far.

Q.—Why din't he get that far? A.—Darned good reason.

Q.—What was it? A.—I shot him.

She Plays Phonograph.

Further answers told the story of her playing the phonograph— "Hula Lou, who had more sweeties than a dog has fleas"—to keep the neighbors from suspecting.

The judge cast unbelieving glances at the young woman who sat so calmly listening to the story of the killing as told in her own words. All this time the jury had been excluded while the judge decided whether the various versions of the killing were to be read before it.

With the return of the jury into the courtroom Beulah "pepped" up a bit and tried to register contrition and regret at the proper intervals.

William F. McLaughlin gave a brief outline of the case the state would present.

Then W. W. O'Brien gave his version and the whole court sat up in attention as he depicted Beulah, the virtuous working girl! Beulah, the modest little housewife! Tears slowly came to Beulah's eyes as he told how Kalstedt, a regular "bum" had come to her apartment early the morning of the shooting, and had tried to borrow a few dollars to get booze. Finally to get rid of him she had given him a dollar, and then that afternoon he had returned, intoxicated, and forced his way in the house.

Frightened, she begged him to leave, but he refused.

Says Beulah Made Mistake.

"And then she foolishly took a drink, just to humor him and get him to go," said Mr. O'Brien with sad regret, "and played the victrola to drown his loud talking. But he started to make love to her, improper advances—and then they took another little drink."

Fascinated, the jury followed him down the path of "another little drink," until Kalstedt threatened to attack her, boasting that he had served time for "having his way with a woman"—"that's the kind of man he was!"

Then, according to her attorney, Beulah, in a frenzy, started—O no, not for the gun, but the telephone, to tell her husband the danger she was in! And it was then Kalstedt went for the gun—conveniently parked on the bed—but she had the inside track! And in the struggle she turned around and that's how he was shot in the back! [Attorney Stewart posed to show just how it was done.]

Later the state called a surprise witness: Mrs. Maybelle Bergman, 1022 Dayton street, head bookkeeper at the laundry where Mrs. Annan was employed.

Q.—Did you hear from Mrs. Annan in the afternoon of April 3— when she was off from work? A.—At about 4:10 she called me up at the office.

Q.—What was said? A.—She said, "Hello, Betty, what are you doing?" and I said, "I'm awfully busy." And she said, "Is Billy there?" meaning Mr. Wilcox. And I said that he'd been in and out. Then she said, "Is Moo there?" meaning Harry Kalstedt. And I answered, "You know he hasn't been here all day long." She said, "That's funny. I had an appointment with him for a quarter after twelve and he hasn't shown up!"

Plays Serenade to Dead.

The court and jury looked at Beulah, for at 4:20 Kalstedt was lying in her apartment—dead—and she was playing the jazz records on the Victrola!

Q.—What did you say then? A.—I said, "What's the matter, Red? You sound kinda stewed." And she said, "No, I haven't had a drink all day. I talk queerly because I'm trying to talk to you and read the telephone directory at the same time." And that was all.

The two women exchanged flashing glances as the pretty brunette stepped down from the witness stand and sailed past "Red."

The character of Harry Kalstedt was brought up in the questioning of W. W. Wilcox. Mr. O'Brien implied that the dead man had been in the penitentiary in Michigan, and the witness resented it.

"He was in the St. Cloud reformatory," Wilcox said.

"For what reason?" the attorney asked.

"Wife desertion," was the answer.

JURY FINDS BEULAH ANNAN IS "NOT GUILTY"

Self-Defense Plea Gains Her Freedom
Thanks Each Member After Verdict.
May 25, 1924, p. 1

By Maurine Watkins.

Beulah Annan, whose pursuit of wine, men, and jazz music was interrupted by her glibness with the trigger finger, was given freedom last night by her "beauty proof" jury.

The jury retired from Judge Lindsay's court at 8:30 and at 10:20 brought in the verdict "Not guilty" on the third ballot, acquitting her of the murder of her admirer, Harry Kalstedt, in her apartment, 817 East 46th street, on April 3. The fair defendant thanked the jury all around, assisted by her faithful husband, Al.

"O, I can't thank you!" she said, flashing a glance at each one as she pressed his hand. "You don't know, you can't know—but I felt sure that you would—" Her appealing glance finished the sentence.

Husband Nearly Overcome.

Mr. Annan, who has stood by her from the very night he found the man lying dead in his bedroom, was almost overcome with joy and gratitude.

"I knew my wife would come through all right!" he said, proudly.

That seemed to be the consensus of opinion.

"Another pretty woman gone free!" was the only comment made by Assistant State's Attorney William F. McLaughlin who prosecuted the case alone after the withdrawal of Roy C. Woods, who was called as a material witness.

Tells Sordid Story.

"Beautiful—but not dumb!"

For she had talked incessantly: two different versions of the shooting before she came to trial, and the third one—when she took the stand yesterday—was the charm.

"We both grabbed for the gun."

Under the glare of motion picture lights—a news weekly—Beulah took the stand. In another new dress—navy twill tied at the side with a childlike moire bow—with new necklace of crystal and jet, she made her debut as an actress. And the jury laughingly nominated the youngest of their sheiks as a Rudolf for the titian haired sheba.

Pleading Eyes on Jury.

More calm than she was Friday, she answered the questions in her childlike southern voice, and turned innocent, pleading eyes to jury and attorney.

Q.—Did you shoot this man? A.—I did.

Q.—Why? A.—Because he was going to shoot me.

Simply she told the story of Kalstedt's morning visit to her apartment, after her husband had gone to work; of his attempt to borrow six dollars from her for booze; and of his subsequent return that afternoon with two quarts of moonshine.

Begged Him to Go.

"I saw he was drunk and begged him to go," she said, "but he refused, and asked me to take a drink first. So I did—just to get him to leave. But still he wouldn't go, though I begged him to, told him my husband might come home and that he would shoot us both."

Q.—And what did he say to that? A.—He said, "To hell with your husband!" Then he insisted that I take another drink and I did. Then he said, "Let's have a little jazz" and we played the Victrola, and then—

She hesitated a moment.

"And then he said, 'Come on into the bedroom' and I refused and begged him to go. And finally I told him"—she faltered and sent an appealing glance to her attorney.

Her Appeal Unheeded.

"Yes?" said Mr. Scott Stewart encouragingly. "Go ahead, Beulah, tell the jury."

She closed her eyes a moment, then went bravely on: "I told him of my—delicate condition. But he refused to believe me—and boasted that another woman had fooled him that way, and that he had done time in the penitentiary for her. And I said, 'You'll do another!' And he

said, 'You'll never send me back!' And I said, 'I'll call my husband!' And
he'll shoot us both!'"

Q.—And what did he say to that? A.—He said, "Where is that—
gun?"

Q.—Then what did he do? A.—He started for the bedroom.

Q.—How did you reach the bedroom? A.—Maybe he was a step
ahead of me. By the time he got to the bed I was even with him—he
grabbed for it, I reached for it and got it first. Then he put up his hand
and said, "By—, I'll kill you yet!"

Tells Details of Shooting.

Q.—Then what did he do? A.—He started toward me, and I pushed
his shoulder with my left hand—and shot.

She closed her eyes—her face pale under the glare of the movie
lights—in horror of the picture, and weakly described the details of the
shooting. She told how she had wiped his face, had turned off the grat-
ing phonograph record, and had sunk down in a daze beside the body.

She denied having called Betty Bergman the afternoon of the murder, told again of her promised immunity if she would make the statements to the police, and denied intimacy with Kalstedt.

Thoroughly poised under direct questioning, she was a trifle non-
plused by the opening attack of the prosecution in cross-questioning,
for Mr. McLaughlin tried to establish the fact that her "story" had been
"framed" by her attorneys. But she rallied when it came to the story
itself, and was only slightly daunted when he pointed out that it was
remarkable that she should be a step behind Kalstedt in the "get-away,"
have the "outside" track, and yet beat him to the gun.

Repudiates Old Statement.

One by one he read her the questions and answers she had made
at the Hyde Park police station the night of the murder, in which she

confessed killing the man after a jealous quarrel. She searched him with her shallow eyes: what was back of it all?

"When you asked this—and was this your answer?" he asked.

"I don't remember."

"No."

"I did not."

One by one she repudiated every statement in the confession, varying the defiance of her "no" with a childishly petulant, "I don't remember."

"That's my story and I'll stick to it," was her attitude—and she did, till she stepped down demurely from the witness stand with the settled complacency of a school girl who has said her piece.

And under the glare of movie lights, Mrs. Mary Neal, her mother, was called by the defense as sympathy witness. Her dark eyes were drawn and mouth set as she answered the few simple questions as to her name, relation to the defendant, etc. Al, her faithful husband, marched briskly to the stand, but was not permitted to testify on account of his relationship.

Testimony in Rebuttal.

Roy C. Woods, originally a prosecutor in the case, was called by the state as a rebuttal witness to refute Mrs. Annan's testimony that he had promised her immunity if she would confess to him.

Q.—Did you state to Beulah Annan that you would help her if she would keep Wilcox's (Kalstedt's brother-in-law) name out of it? A.—I did not.

Q.—Did you tell her it was no crime for her to shoot a man in her own house? A.—Most certainly not.

Q.—Did you tell her that she couldn't "frame" anything with you? A.—I did.

Beulah sat with bowed head through the state's opening argument, in which Mr. McLaughlin pointed out the weak points in her story: that a woman should try to "soothe" a man who was threatening to attack her by drinking with him; that he knew where the gun was—in a totally strange house; that he was shot in the back.

"You have seen that face, gentlemen. It's probable that she hadn't had many men tell her to 'go to hell,' and that was why she went for the gun!" the prosecutor told the jury.

His main argument was hinged on the credibility of the witness, who had made three entirely different statements to the jury.

Beulah in Tears.

William Scott Stewart read line by line the confessions and demonstrated the third degree methods that were used to obtain them. Then Beulah, the tender hearted slayer, broke into gentle sobs. She had played the victrola while the man she murdered lay dying, she had laughed at his inquest, she had sat calm and composed while they read descriptions of the crime, but she broke down when she heard her attorney's impassioned account of the suffering she had undergone at the hands of the police and assistant state's attorneys, who questioned her for statements.

And again she was overcome with emotion when Mr. O'Brien painted the picture of "this frail little girl, gentlemen, struggling with a drunken brute"—and the jury shook their heads in approbation and chewed their gum more energetically.

"The verdict is in your hands," was the voice of the peoples' prosecutor, "and you must decide whether you will permit a woman to commit a crime and let her go because she is good looking; you must decide whether you want to let another pretty woman go out and say 'I got away with it!'"

And they did.

MRS. GAERTNER HAS "CLASS" AS SHE FACES JURY

Demure but with an "Air" at Murder Trial.
June 4, 1924, p. 4

By Maurine Watkins.

Belva Gaertner, charged with the murder of Walter Law, was a "perfect lady" yesterday in Judge Lindsay's court as she faced four of the jurors who will decide whether she really did shoot the young auto salesman, found dead in her sedan March 12.

For the lady herself was so "dead drunk" after a night of gin and jazz at the Gingham Inn that she doesn't remember!

And another woman studied the jurors, a sweet-faced woman in heavy mourning; Mrs. Walter Law, who did not know Belva existed till they met at the slain man's inquest, and of the two she seemed more concerned.

Twice a Divorcee.

Cabaret dancer and twice divorcee, Mrs. Gaertner was as demure as any convent girl—yesterday!—with brown eyes dreamily cast downward. Her lips were closed in a not-quite smile, the contour of her cheek was unbroken by lines, and rejuvenating rouge made her well on the dangerous side of 30.

"Say, she's got the Annan girl skinned a mile!" said one ardent court fan.

"Not so pretty, but more class," said another.

"Class"—that was Belva. For she lived up to her reputation as "the most stylish" of murderess' row: a blue twill suit bound with black braid, and white lacy frill down the front; patent leather slippers with shimmering French heels, chiffon gun metal hose. And a hat—ah, that hat!

helmet shaped, with a silver buckle and cockade of ribbon, with one streamer tied jauntily—coquettishly—bewitchingly—under her chin.

This Man Hat Proof.

"Would you let a stylish hat make you find her 'not guilty'?" Asst. State's Attorney Samuel Hamilton asked a prospective juror.

He staunchly answered, "No," and solemnly agreed that "sex" should have no part in his verdict.

Mrs. Gaertner spoke only once—a whisper to her attorney, Thomas Nash. Then he asked the jurors: "Would you be prejudiced if it should develop that—er—the lady had been drinking that evening?"

The prospective jurors assured him that they wouldn't, and the questioning went merrily on to find a hat-proof, sex-proof, and "damp" jury, who would also accept circumstantial evidence as conclusive.

No Witnesses to Shooting.

For there were no witnesses: just a man found dead, slumped over the steering wheel of Mrs. Gaertner's car; a bullet in his head from her pistol left lying on the sedan floor; and the woman herself in her apartment at 4809 Forrestville avenue—hysterical, disheveled, and drenched with blood.

She is expected to take the stand in her own behalf, and the defense—loss of memory—will at least be unique.

"She's as guilty as Kitty Malm," said Assistant State's Attorney Harry Pritzker, who won a verdict of "life" against the "tiger girl," "and I hope to send her over the same road."

Have Alternative Count.

The state, thus far, has not qualified the jurors for the death sentence, though they indicated it may be asked later. A charge of manslaughter is also included in the indictment, so that if the state fails to show "intent to kill" she may be found guilty on the lesser charge.

The four jurymen accepted were: Francis Parker, 923 East 55th street; John G. Keenan, 3500 Adams street; Robert Freeman, 4316 North Springfield avenue; M. M. Eaton, 746 Addison street.

STATE LAUNCHES TRIAL OF BELVA FOR LAW KILLING

Dancer Faces Jury in Fashion's Latest.
June 5, 1924, p. 12

Belva Gaertner, the lady who was "so drunk she doesn't remember," registered virtuous calm as the state opened its case yesterday in an attempt to prove her guilty of murdering Walter Law.

Her sultry eyes never lost their dreaminess as policemen described the dead body slumped over the wheel of her Nash sedan—the matted hair around the wound, the blood that dripped in pools—and her revolver and "fifth" of gin lying on the floor. Her sensuous mouth kept its soft curves as they told of finding her in her apartment—4809 Forrestville avenue—with blood on coat, blood on her dress of green velvet and silver cloth, and blood on the silver slippers.

Calm and poised—but her slim French-heeled shoes beat the floor, twitched nervously, and crossed and re-crossed themselves.

Springer First Witness.

Those twinkling feet had danced her into Overbeck's heart, when she was Belle Brown, cabaret girl; that had carried her to—and from!—a bridle path romance with Gaertner, wealthy manufacturer; that had stolen her into a "palship" with a young married man—and then to a murder trial.

The opening statement for the prosecution was made by Assistant State's Attorney Samuel Hamilton; that for the defense was waived by Nash and Ahern, and Marshall Solberg. Dr. Joseph Springer, coroner's physician, was called as first witness for the state.

He testified to examining the body at 4:55 the morning of March 12, and stated that there were no powder burns near the wound where the bullet had entered near the right temple. "A gun must be held within fifteen inches or so to make powder burns," he explained.

Scoffs at Suicide Theory.

"From the absence of these, is it your opinion that he did not shoot himself?" asked Mr. Hamilton.

"He did not," was the answer.

In cross-questioning, Michael Ahern, counsel for the defense, tried to get the doctor to place the pistol at the presumed angle and distance, while he posed as Law committing suicide. He clicked the revolver.

"There! You see, he could have killed himself!" said Mr. Ahern.

"He could not!" answered Dr. Springer crisply.

He also identified the gin bottle which was found lying on the floor of the car. Belva's jury, selected for their lack of prejudice in favor of the Volstead act, pepped up a bit at sight of this, and Belva herself leaned forward. But it was empty.

Sergt. Quinn and Patrolman Fitzgerald told of finding the dead body and of tracing the owner of the car by the license number. Detective William Sullivan went to the owner's address, he said, and found Mrs. Gaertner, in a bath robe, with the blood drenched clothes on the floor.

She couldn't shake her head nor nod approvingly at the testimony, for she doesn't "remember," but she could show impatience as the officer floundered in describing her clothes. But—to his relief—they were admitted in evidence; the mashed hat and rumpled coat, the "one more struggle and I'm free" dress, and the flimsy slippers.

Describe Café Scene.

According to Dr. Springer and the police officers Mrs. Gaertner, when they talked to her, was sober early that morning. Bert Brown, floorman of the Gingham Inn, was also called to prove this point. He said that Law and Mrs. Gaertner had come to the inn, at 68th street and Cottage Grove avenue, five or six times previous to the night of the shooting, and that evening had arrived about 10 o'clock and stayed an hour and a half.

According to his statement, the Gingham Inn is matched in dryness only by the Sahara; no liquor is sold there, no liquor is brought there, no liquor is displayed there on table, floor, or under cover. Consequently the couple, who arrived sober, must have left in the same condition.

"You're saying that to protect the place where you're employed!" flared the counsel for the defense.

The statement Mrs. Gaertner had made at the police station early that morning was ruled out by Judge Lindsay, but Sergeant William Egan testified as to the points she had been questioned on.

"She said Law was at her house at 9 o'clock that night," he said, "and when they left for the Gingham inn she got her ex-husband's gun, for fear of a hold-up, and put it in the pocket of the car."

With similar aplomb, Mrs. Gaertner, most "stylish" of Murderess' Row, fastened her "choker," gathered up her white kid gloves as court was adjourned, and swept out.

JURY FINDS MRS. GAERTNER NOT GUILTY

Verdict Found After Eight Ballots.
June 6, 1924, p. 1

By Maurine Watkins.

Belva Gaertner, another of those women who messed things up by adding a gun to her fondness for gin and men, was acquitted last night at 12:10 o'clock of the murder of Walter Law. "So drunk she didn't remember" whether she shot the man found dead in her sedan at Forrestville avenue and 50th street March 12—

But after six and one-half hours and eight ballots the jury said she didn't.

Mrs. Gaertner lost the emotionless poise she maintained throughout the trial, burst into hysterical laughter, threw her arms around her attorneys, and thanked the jury.

"O, I'm so happy!" she exclaimed over and over, "so happy! And I want to hurry out now and get some air!"

Prepares at Once to Leave.

She left at once to get her elaborate wardrobe from the jail, and from there went home with her sister, Mrs. Charles Kruschaar. Some time within the next month, she said, she will re-marry her divorced husband, William Gaertner, the wealthy manufacturer, and they will sail for Europe "to forget all this."

But there's a woman who won't forget: Mrs. Freda Law, widow of the slain man, who half fainted when the verdict was read and crept away to sob in the arms of her sister: "There's no justice in Illinois! No justice! Walter paid—why shouldn't she?"

"Women—just women!" was the laconic comment of Assistant State's Attorney Harry Pritzker.

"Why did they take so long?" said the crowd.

Long Wait for Verdict.

That's what Belva Gaertner asked herself as she smoked cigarets and paced the floor of the "bullpen" while the jury, not six feet away, deliberated whether she had murdered Walter Law, found dead in her sedan March 12.

And neither they nor the blasé divorcée, Cook county's most stylish defendant, knew that Judge Lindsay had ruled when the defense asked for nolle prosse: "I haven't the power to tell the state's attorney what to do, and therefore deny the motion. But if the jury should bring in a verdict of guilty, I am confident the Supreme court would reverse the decision, as the evidence is only circumstantial: strong enough to arouse suspicion of guilt but not to convict."

Defense Waives Argument.

"The state has not made its case," was the attitude of the defense, represented by Nash & Ahern, and Marshall Solberg, who waived their opening statement, rested without offering a single witness and waived closing argument.

The jury, who had heard only the state's plea for "a just verdict," listened gravely, and the court fans sleepily, to the instructions of the judge with their droning rhythm: ". . . beyond all reasonable doubt . . . you shall find the defendant not guilty . . ."

But they all sat alert when he reached the age of the defendant: "about 38," and turned to stare at the slim, youthfully rounded creature who'd never looked prettier.

She's Stylishly Dressed.

And she wore a new dress—café au lait, braided in black, with bell shaped sleeves and deep cuffs—that clung in soft folds to her body. And the cloche hat of a deeper brown matched her eyes, and the mink "choker" softened the lines of her throat. Only her hands with their rosily tinted nails showed her age—and nervousness, as she played with her gloves and fur while the state attempted early in the day again to prove she was not "too drunk to remember."

Alfred Quodbach, proprietor of the Gingham Inn at 6800 Cottage Grove avenue, and his head waiter, William F. Leathers, testified concerning the sobriety of Law and Mrs. Gaertner while they were in the café the night he was killed.

"Perfectly sober," was Quodbach's statement.

"I wish I had always been as sober as they were that night!" said Leathers.

Following testimony by the widow, Mrs. Freda Law establishing corpus delicti, the case went to the jury.

MURDERESS ROW LOSES CLASS AS BELVA IS FREED

But Four Obscure "Girl" Killers in Jail.
June 7, 1924, p. 10

"Not guilty" for Belva Gaertner, who was acquitted yesterday of the murder of Walter Law, brought joy to her playmates in the county jail, and made hope spring a little higher in the hearts of the remaining women "killers."

Only Sabella Nitti mourned. Poor Sabella! who chopped her husband up one day, assisted by a roomer, the state charges. Her greeting to visitors used to be: "Me choke"—which being interpreted reads: "I'm sentenced to hang"—and now she waits a new trial. Each acquittal brings pangs of comparison to her.

"She have gun. She shoot. She go free. Me; no gun, no shoot; me here over a year!"

Only Four Left.

Only four women, the fewest in years, are now waiting trial for murder—for they're getting out even faster than they're getting in! And the two who walked to freedom in the last two weeks, "pretty" Beulah Annan and "stylish" Belva Gaertner, robbed the women's quarters of their claims to distinction and plunged murderess' row into oblivion.

Two of those left are colored: Minnie Nichols and Rose Epps. The other two, Sabella Nitti and Lela Foster, are middle aged and—well, neither is cursed with the grace or the beauty of Diana. Then, too, Beulah and Belva killed young men friends, and these ladies only "bumped off" their husbands.

So they can't hope for publicity, maybe not even acquittal. They'll be given the same chance with the "weapons of defense" that the other women have had: powder, rouge, lipstick, and mascara. Makeup is taboo in jail, only soap and water is permitted, until those testing days when they face the "twelve good men and true."

Then the Fashion Show.

Then begins the fashion show, for each woman is firmly convinced that clothes make the man look more sympathetically. Shops send dresses on approval, friends bring in frocks of their own, and anxious lawyers borrow from their wives for their clients. They study every effect, turn, and change—and who can say it's time wasted?

But these "girls" will lack the advice of Belva, known even in some other circles as an expert in dress.

"The place ain't the same without her," they mourn, for she was the best dancer, the best card player among them.

It's true she was a little—well, not industrious, and hired the other girls to wash out her clothes and iron them "on the wall." She let Sabella take care of her neat little bunk—but that's over now and they wish her happiness on her European trip to "forget it all."

Third Time a Charm.

"Funny the way they take it," mused one girl. "Soon as Beulah was out she up and left poor Al cold and flat; and now Belva rushes off to a wedding!"

"Married him once, and that was annulled; married him again and got a divorce; third time's charm!"

Mrs. Gaertner, who is resting up for a few days with her sister, Mrs. Charles Kurschaar, at 4457 North Spaulding avenue, said yesterday that no definite date had been set for the wedding nor for their sailing—"some time within the next month," was all she said.

A terrible strain, she declared, but she looks a hundred per cent better after her three months' "rest cure" in jail!

Notes

1. Gaertner's first name was changed here from that of the first article because "Belva" was her legal name; "Belle" was only her stage name. The conversion of Law's first name from "Robert" in Watkins's first report to "Walter" simply corrected a mistake.

2. The break that occurs at this point is a printing error. Apparently the typesetter overlooked or dropped a line of text.

3. This shift in Beulah's age from twenty-eight, given in the previous report, corrected another of Watkins's errors.

4. Another printing error—"here" should have been "her."

5. Again the typesetter either overlooked or dropped a line of text.

6. In the previous accounts, Watkins consistently spelled the victim's name "Kolstedt." The change here to "Kohlstedt" may have been a misspelling, but since it was subsequently changed to "Kalstedt" for the trial, Watkins was probably trying to correct an initial mistake, which was not accomplished until she saw the legal documents for the trial.

7. This alteration of Unkafer's age from 46 in the previous article was either an oversight or a correction.

Thomas H. Pauly is a professor of American literature at the University of Delaware. For ten years, he served as the director of the American Studies Program. He is the author of *An American Odyssey: Elia Kazan and American Culture* as well as numerous articles on American literature, theater, film, and popular culture. He is currently writing a critical study on crime as entertainment focusing on the fictionalization of crime during the 1920s.